WHO KILLED MY BANK

CHAITANYA

INDIA • SINGAPORE • MALAYSIA

Notion Press

No. 8, 3rd Cross Street,
CIT Colony, Mylapore,
Chennai, Tamil Nadu – 600 004

First Published by Notion Press 2021
Copyright © Chaitanya 2021
All Rights Reserved.

ISBN 978-1-63669-621-8

This book has been published with all efforts taken to make the material error-free after the consent of the author. However, the author and the publisher do not assume and hereby disclaim any liability to any party for any loss, damage, or disruption caused by errors or omissions, whether such errors or omissions result from negligence, accident, or any other cause.

While every effort has been made to avoid any mistake or omission, this publication is being sold on the condition and understanding that neither the author nor the publishers or printers would be liable in any manner to any person by reason of any mistake or omission in this publication or for any action taken or omitted to be taken or advice rendered or accepted on the basis of this work. For any defect in printing or binding the publishers will be liable only to replace the defective copy by another copy of this work then available.

Sketches by Swamy, Toronto
E: isomas@live.com
W: themanojava.com

Dedicated to

"Millions of depositors who trust their banks and need to know whether they are secure and sound for safekeeping their hard-earned savings"

CONTENTS

Foreword *9*
Acknowledgement *15*
Preface *21*

1. The Gory Details 25
   - The Disclosure 27
   - Run Up to the Hearing 33
   - The Case Begins 37
   - The Role of the Chairman and
     the Board Tumbles Out 41
   - One Man Show 63
   - The Willing CEO 73
   - The Great Compromising Act 79
   - Regulator Blinks and
     Tries to Pass the Buck 83

- The Muck Runs Deeper 87
- Media Keeps Up the Momentum..............89
- Damage Control – Too Little, Too Late....93
- Sample of Fraudulent Loan Cases 101

2. The Tales of Human Tragedy, Each Different from the Other Yet Inextricably Interwoven 111

- A Marriage Stops..113
- Home Business Gets Killed Before It Starts...117
- Shattering of a Mother's Dream 121
- Life Savings of An NRI Wiped Out 127
- Worthy Son is Forced to Fail in His Duty...133
- Good Samaritan Employer Halts His Yearly Gesture 141
- Actress Pawns Her Jewels to Pay the Grocer...147
- Housing Society's Redevelopment Plans Get Stalled 155
- Senior Citizen is Made to Beg for Medicines..163
- Hospital Trust's Funds Get Blocked.......169
- Self-Help Group (SHG) Loses Deposits of 'Below Poverty Line' Members 173

- Community Gets a Rude Shock Excommunicates Top Officials 183
- In a Triple Whammy, Senior Citizen Loses Everything 191
- Students the Worst Hit 199
- Employees Find Themselves in a Catch 22 Situation 207
- No Takers for the Tainted Assets 219

3. **Tips to Customers While Selecting a Bank** **227**
4. **Suggested Steps for the Regulator's Consideration** **251**

Banking Abbreviations 271
About the Author 285

FOREWORD

Unlike elephants we, the people, do not have long memories. That explains why and how people get fooled exactly in the same manner, repeatedly. If only people were to remember the scary and unfortunate events of their lives, where they were taken for a ride by individuals or institutions, people would be more cautious and not be naïve enough to be fooled time and again.

WKMB is the work of a consummate banker with an eye for detail, who on the strength of his vast experience in the banking industry, has been able to weave a story that is chillingly real and frightening, yet informative. The reader is being provided with an accurate account of what generally goes wrong in a bank that collapses and takes with it the savings, dreams and aspirations of thousands, if not millions, of its customers.

WKMB offers remarkable insight to a layman in unravelling the mystery of banking. The entire woven web of banking has been carefully separated and laid bare in a simple textbook format for the benefit of the uninitiated reader, students of banking and for the millions of bank customers.

The deceit and the scam unleashed on the depositors is explained in an objective manner with the precision of a surgeon, and without getting unduly patronising. The end result is a book that educates both a seasoned investor and a layman alike.

While explaining some of the complex concepts, the writer, bends down to the level of the most ignorant readers, so that they easily understand his painstakingly granular analysis of each aspect of banking.

As a banker myself, I could easily identify with the various events that unfolded one after the other in WKMB. I am sure even a non-banker will find it easy to understand the various aspects of banking or what goes in the name of banking at some of the banks. The readers will find WKMB to be a page turner and would want to read it cover to cover in one sitting. While the entire book can be completed in a few hours or over a weekend, the insight and tips given in its pages will last the reader an entire lifetime. The incriminating information captured in these few hundred pages is simply staggering, and can be an effective guide in the hands of the common public and the depositors alike.

Though there are bankers who may have a rich and vast experience, there are few who could clearly articulate their experiences, as has been done in WKMB. The readers also get a glimpse of Mumbai, the Financial Capital of the Country, and the various types of people, many of them migrants, inhabiting the city of dreams and making it big through sheer hard work and perseverance. The reader is taken around the city in an R K Narayan or V S Naipaul-esque manner, the only difference being that WKMB is not about a fictional city, but is set in the country's melting-pot, the most vibrant, resilient to a fault, strikingly fair, just and cosmopolitan city. The city means business, and does not ignore those with merit and a burning desire to make it big. In its pages, the writer demonstrates a keen sense of observation and a knowledge of the lanes and by-lanes of the city that never sleeps, like the back of his hand. His love for the city and the vast majority of the city's common folk who shape the city's character and growth, is well-captured.

During my discussions with Chaitanya, I could notice his pain and anguish about the various banks' failures and fallouts. He felt it was not at all fair to the depositors. He would say that for every one customer whose deposit has got stuck, there are at least four others who are affected as they were dependent on the depositor. The many deaths that happened in vain are inexplicable and unpardonable. He mentioned that during his visit to the many homes and the small and medium business establishments that got affected due to banks' failures, he observed human misery of a mammoth proportion that defied logic. Each one of the nearly million customers of the banks were hard working people minding their own business and hence, it was complete injustice to them. Everyone seemed to have a unique story to narrate, full of human misery, grief, and unimaginable pathos.

Though he wanted to write about each customer he had met, there were times, he said, when he could simply not put into words the sorrow and despair felt by the customers. With a heavy heart, he locked up many of such stories in his heart and could bring himself to write only about a few of their experiences. These cases are representative of the large-scale damage and will give the reader an idea of the massive impact banks' failures have had on the life of hard working people and their families across the society.

I am sure readers will find WKMB enlightening at different levels. I am happy to write this foreword for a book that has its soul and heart in the right place, and is empathetic to the depositors' interests.

WKMB, in my opinion, will play an important role in educating the common people of the country, non-bankers, and the present and prospective depositors of banks from getting cheated by some of the banks, which have thrown caution to the wind and seem to have taken their customers for granted. In that sense, it is a must read for all bank depositors to become more informed and discerning. It is especially relevant to those who place their high value deposits without performing a due diligence of the financial health of the bank.

The book is smartly divided into five sections, each logically connected with the other and, at the same time, maintaining a new thread. Readers will find that the book follows a pattern and a natural flow. Like all good reference books, the reader could choose to read any section or topic without going through the previous thread.

WKMB is an eye opener and can be considered to be a true reflection of banking and bankers. I would strongly recommend WKMB to the common public, the students of banking, and to all those professional bankers, who like, medical practitioners, are performing an essential service of maintaining the financial health of their respective banks, their customers and the society. WKMB will help these bankers introspect and undertake important course corrections, take a relook at their belief systems, as may be required, to serve their bank and its customers. They would well realise their duty to serve with integrity and without fear or favour to the best of their abilities in a fast changing India, where knowledge and expectations of the customers are undergoing an irreversible metamorphosis.

Finally, I can say that Chaitanya is in the mould of a true crusader, writing for the cause of the unknown depositor who may get cheated if similar bank failures continue to occur.

Vijaya, Ex Banker

ACKNOWLEDGEMENT

Who Killed My Bank (WKMB) had to be written. The circumstances and the events of the past year with two large banks, one catering to the customers in the middle and lower strata of the society while the other serving the well-heeled, savvy customers, collapsing in quick succession, back to back, compelled me to put pen to the paper. Besides, as a banker with four decades of experience with various banks in India and abroad, it was my duty to share with my readers the knowledge and insight that I happened to gain during my long career. Enlightening the readers is, I believe, my way of serving the interests of customers, who seem to place their unflinching and sometimes blind trust in an entity just because it has the word 'bank' attached to its name.

While WKMB will be of interest to the customers of all banks, it will be specifically relevant to the customers who invest their hard earned income and life savings with some of the little known banks just because they offer personalised services and slightly better returns on deposits. Facilitating these customers to take informed decisions diligently, based on hard facts, is the main objective of WKMB – a labour of my love for the noble profession of banking. If I am able to help even a few hundred customers to invest safely and smartly without getting conned, I would consider that my aim in writing WKMB has been achieved.

I could elucidate my thoughts mainly because I had a ringside view of what was going on at many of the professional banks, where I got an opportunity to associate and undertake consulting assignments.

Critical information is not easily accessible to the ordinary customers or even to most of the employees working in a bank. The non-transparent working style adopted by some of the banks and the economical manner in which they share information purely on a "need to know" basis with their team members, was one more reason for me to write WKMB and share the observations and finer points with my readers.

I personally faced and lived through many of the instances cited in WKMB, while handling process improvement assignments at some of the finest of banks that desired to embrace change and imbibe best practices.

My work and assignments enabled me to view, from close quarters, the motivations that drive the Management and Board at some of these banks. To put it mildly, many a times, I was aghast with the way the key stakeholder and safe keepers of trust at some of these banks seemed to have treated such public institutions as if they were their family fiefdom or personal piggy banks to draw or divert money at their whim and fancy, with utter impunity and without an iota of guilt or concern for the ultimate interests of the thousands of depositors, who had parted with their life-savings and placed their complete and unequivocal trust on such banks.

I feel it is only appropriate to dedicate this book to the millions of hard working and innocent common people, who trust banks as custodians of their life savings, only to receive a rude shock when they get duped, due to the misdeeds of a few unscrupulous bankers in power, who bring disrepute to the fine profession of banking, the very engine of the economy.

I thank my Parents who have always encouraged me and my sisters and brothers to excel in our chosen fields and work towards achieving our full potential. I also thank my school and college teachers for instilling sound values in me. I thank my wife, son, daughter, daughter-in-law, son-in-law and my extended family members, many of whom have been fine career bankers themselves, for prodding me to write WKMB and share my insights for the benefit of the uninitiated depositors and the general readers.

I specially thank my wife for helping me with editing this book and ensuring that the language used throughout the book is kept simple, and the style conversational, so that it is easy to read and follow. I also thank my friends, all of whom are wonderful and passionate bankers, with whom I was fortunate to be associated during my long journey.

WKMB, which is a fusion of fact and fiction, would not have been possible without the support and encouragement of so many family members, friends, colleagues and well-wishers, who felt it was most appropriate to bring out a book on the dos and don'ts, as well as the many pitfalls and land mines to be avoided in the financial ecosystem, when deciding which bank to consider while investing one's hard-earned savings. If I have missed out, inadvertently, to mention the name of anyone in particular, I wish to be excused for the same.

The names of the various characters and institutions have been modified to protect their identity.

There are no individual protagonists or antagonists. For this reason, names of the institutions and individuals have not been mentioned. This is also done to avoid sensationalising the book and to be able to achieve a larger purpose of carefully focussing on a greater cause of cleaning up the mess, thereby seeking to rebuild the trust deficit of the entire sector, rather than merely concentrating on demonising the act of one particular entity or individual.

PREFACE

Today, where news about a bank's failure or folding up at some place in our country has become a common occurrence, there seems to be a justification for the lack of trust amongst customers while dealing with some of the banks. The anxiety of the depositors gets aggravated when the news filters about restrictions placed by the regulator on some bank or the other in the country. The print, electronic and social networking platforms ensure that information and, sometimes, panic and mis-information gets disseminated far and wide within minutes. In today's social networking environment, the reaction time to contain the fallout or offer clarification is too short, before the irreparable damage gets unleashed within hours.

Few rotten apples in any system can result in a cascading effect to the detriment of other well-meaning players in the industry. Banking is no exception to this universal truth. In the recent months, banking seems to have lost its halo and, with it, the friendly banker seems to have gained notoriety and the mistrust of his customers. The recent events have wiped the smile from the face of customers and have greatly contributed to the increase in their stress levels, loss of wealth, business and peace of mind.

WKMB can also be considered as a self-help book for any individual and/or customer of banks, pan India. It is written in a simple and easy to understand language, without using financial jargons or complicated phrases. The aim in writing WKMB is to assist customers to take an informed decision before they decide to invest their hard earned money with a bank or a similar financial institution.

In today's uncertain times, it is difficult to meet our daily needs while simultaneously saving for the future of our family. Today, we seem to be getting cheated with the return on our Savings and Fixed Deposits, with the rate of inflation (cost of living) exceeding the rate of interest on Savings Account and Fixed Deposits. Though there are many avenues for savings, each comes with a risk - return combination. For a lay person, whether in employment or a profession, someone about to retire or a senior citizen depending largely on the fixed monthly interest income, it gets very complicated at times to assess and analyse various investment options.

Those who are no longer young or have a limited risk appetite to invest in the equity market, take the easy route of investing in bank fixed deposits for fixed monthly returns, despite the falling interest rates on deposits. This investor class, many a times, get attracted to a bank paying few additional basis points of interest, in comparison to the other banks in the vicinity.

WKMB neither castigates nor recommends any bank in particular. It also does not engage in a debate on whether a Public Sector Bank is better vis-à-vis a Foreign, Private or a Co-operative Bank. These are non-issues, since, to the customer of any bank filing for liquidation, the amount of insurance cover on their deposit made available by The Deposit Insurance Credit Guarantee Corporation (DICGC) is just the same, irrespective of the type of bank they have their deposits with.

Ultimately, in a market driven economy, when a bank collapses, the customers are required to fend for themselves. There are no instant solutions to resolve the woes of the depositors of a failed bank. Thus, there is no other better option for the customers than to be well-informed. Being ignorant and not doing their basic research is no excuse for getting conned later by a Ponzi scheme or losing money at a bank on the verge of a collapse, whatever be the compulsions or temptations of the depositors to park their funds with such banks.

WKMB attempts to demystify and help customers understand the various aspects of banking and what they should look for in a bank before investing their hard earned money. In other words, WKMB separates the chaff from the grain, by educating the customers in an easy and step by step manner.

It is clearly brought out in the various pages of WKMB that it is always the Customers and Depositors, who are ultimately required to pay a heavy price with their entire life savings itself, for falling prey to the temptation of earning a little more interest on their deposits to beat inflation/cost of living.

The Gory Details

SECTION 01

1

THE DISCLOSURE

"I, the MD of your bank, regret to inform that from today your bank has been put under regulatory restriction under sec 35A of The Banking Regulation Act, by RBI, for a period of 6 months, due to irregularities voluntarily disclosed to RBI. As MD of the bank, I take full responsibility, and assure all the depositors that the irregularities will be rectified before the expiry of 6 months. All efforts are being made to remove the restrictions by rectifying the irregularities. I know it is a difficult time for all of you and any apology may not restore the pain you are undergoing. Please co-operate with us. We assure you that we will definitely overcome this situation and stand strong."

This terse submission was to become the inflection point in the history of banking in India, setting a tone for innumerable regulatory directions, and go on to change the face of banking in the country forever.

The cryptic message was ignored and mistaken by thousands of illiterate or semi-literate customers of the Bank as yet another marketing message from their bank. Little did they know that the message conveyed by the MD was going to sound a death knell for many of them. The message on their mobile phone was going to irreversibly alter their life forever.

The message from the MD was a play of words, designed to showcase how transparent and virtuous the bank had been in 'voluntarily' disclosing the irregularities on its own and, by doing so, it was coming clean and helping the regulator and other agencies discover the many lapses that they themselves had failed to detect all these years. The unstated and implied message was that the bank had been functioning in a questionable manner and was successfully getting away with it all these years.

So, what forced the sudden change of heart at the top echelon of the bank? Was it an inner voice of the top management to redeem itself or simply a realisation that their game was up? The trigger, seemingly, was the decision of another bank to knock on the doors of The National Company Law Tribunal (NCLT) in a bid to recover dues from the very same corporate group to which the failed bank had also lent its maximum loans. This turn of events seemed to be the tipping point, as all the banks that had lent to the defaulting corporate entity had to disclose their respective credit exposure to the regulator.

It was a do or die situation for all the banks as they had no option but to confirm their exposure to the stressed corporate entity.

Was it due to the tightening of the noose around the neck of the corporate group by multiple lenders, that prompted the MD and the top management of the bank to come clean, or was it that the regulator, in any case, was about to unearth massive wrongdoings at the bank on the verge of failure, courtesy the whistle blowers' meeting with the regulator? It was not immediately clear. The mysterious cause and effect would take many months to unravel.

Yet, regardless of the reasons and compulsions on the part of the MD to lay bare various omissions and commissions of the bank, the lives of tens of thousands of its loyal depositors would eventually turn upside down forever. The event would go on to prove to be a watershed moment, and become a thorn in the flesh of the regulator. It would end up shaking the very confidence of millions in the nation's banking industry.

As details were to emerge in the coming weeks and months, the MD's message, in retrospect, turned out to be a feeble and failed attempt to reassure the depositors and buy time.

The bank was caught in an inextricable web of its own making and was doomed to collapse, with over 70% of its loans to a single related party of dubious reputation and a questionable business model. The debt ridden and over leveraged corporate entity found its business becoming unsustainable in a country that was taking steps to engage in a massive clean-up, in an all out effort to stake a claim to the world to get recognised as a transparent economy and a preferred investment grade destination.

Unfortunately, the bank's staff and innocent customers were paying the price of the bank's top management's inability to realise the winds of change blowing in the country and embrace the change in time. They continued to conduct their affairs in the same traditional manner, with little or no respect for governance, compliance and standard operating procedures. The bank kept lending to the defaulting corporate group, much against the prudential norms that are mandated by the regulators to be followed by all banks.

Additionally, it was to be revealed in later investigations that the bank was acting negligently and not in good faith, by knowingly doing business with the ill-gotten wealth of some of its top notch customers. It was proving to be a nexus and the perfect recipe for massive financial fraud that was destined to result in the imminent collapse of the bank.

The MD's message, surely made at the behest of his handlers, the Chairman and Board of Directors, sounded fake and hollow. In hindsight, the message and the press meet that followed, showed how naïve the bank's management was in not realising that their misadventure had spiralled out of their hands, assuming the proportion of a financial Frankenstein. In its wake, it was to destroy the financial health, reputation and goodwill of thousands of stakeholders associated with the bank. The bank was soon to find itself going down deeper, in a quicksand of sorts, unable to extricate itself from the mess of its own making.

2

RUN UP TO THE HEARING

The ornate, gothic styled Room 15 in the Bombay High Court was big enough to comfortably accommodate nearly hundred observers. However, considering the interest that this case had generated over the past six months, with nearly Sixty deaths during the period, the crowd that had gathered to hear the arguments and counter arguments was so large that even Room 15 seemed to be small, stuffy and congested.

There were several twists and turns culminating in the run-up to the hearing of one of the most sensational cases in recent times. Initially, the case was to be heard by the senior-most Judge, but later, owing to the sensitive nature of the case, a three-member bench was appointed to decide.

Eventually, even that option was set aside, with two of the judges recusing themselves from hearing the case.

A Public Interest Litigation filed by few, was later converted to a class action suit signed by hundreds of depositors as petitioners. The same was promptly admitted by the court.

In a clear departure from established practice, after nearly sixty years since the abolition of the Jury system in the country, it was felt in the legal circles that the case was fit enough for the arguments to be heard, documentary evidence to be perused, witnesses to be cross-examined and judgement to be pronounced by jury members, consisting of those from various vocations and drawn from different walks of life. Several luminaries saw merit in such a submission, as the case had affected the monetary status, peace of mind, and dignity of more than a million customers of the bank. This made it desirable, as an exception, to deviate from the past, and consider the case to be heard and judgement to be collectively delivered by the jury, consisting of randomly selected common people. It was seen as a form of poetic justice.

However, the court in its wisdom, finally constituted a five-member bench, along with experienced bankers to explain finer points and clarify doubts, if any, that the bench might seek.

Also, for the first time, journalists from print and electronic media were allowed to cover the proceedings with certain mandatory requirements to maintain decorum and peace in the courtroom, so as to ensure that not a word of what the prosecution and defense attorneys uttered would be missed. It was fast turning out to be the most followed case in recent memory.

3

THE CASE BEGINS

It was a charged atmosphere, where the high and mighty from the world of banking and finance, the corporate bigwigs, movie moguls, political heavyweights, officials from the regulatory and enforcement agencies, along with the affected parties cutting across economic and social divide, were to be called in for questioning and cross examination by the prosecution and defense counsel to assess the reasons for the bank's failure and its impact of the massive fallout.

The case itself seemed to be a great leveller, as it had shaken and uniformly affected all those unsuspecting customers who had reposed trust in the institution whose very basis for business was to uphold the trust of its depositors. The case had thus brought together on a single platform the likes of President and the Peon, the Socialite and the Social Worker, the Informed and the Illiterate, the High Heeled and those from the Bottom of the pyramid in our society.

With each passing day, for over six months, the case had gathered steady momentum and attention of both the national and international media. It was a case that affected over a million middle and lower income customers, who had blindly trusted the bank, licensed by various agencies and the regulator to be fit enough to park their life savings. The depositors had no reason to believe that their bank would prove everyone wrong and go bust.

A list of all the accused and co-accused within the bank and outside was drawn up. Summons were sent to them, to appear before the court. On arriving at the court, their personal and official mobile phones were confiscated as per the standard procedure.

This seemingly innocuous first step was enough to unsettle most of the accused, and conveyed a clear message that the court meant business right away. Even those who generally maintained a calm façade could get a mild jolt to crack them up or expect what was coming.

Starting with the Chairman of the Board, the entire Board of Directors was called in, one by one, to depose before the court, and to explain their academic qualifications, how they had got elected as Board members, the number of share-holders that were eligible to cast their votes during the bank's election, the records of notices that were sent to all the eligible share-holders inviting them for the election vis-à-vis the actual number of voters, in percentage terms, who came in to cast their votes, the names of all the candidates and their backgrounds, the votes polled by each one of them, the winning margin, the observations made by the returning officer deputed from the Registrar's office as presiding officer at the election, etc. All details were examined in a threadbare manner.

Similarly, the Secretary to the Board was questioned on the various regulatory provisions followed or disregarded by the bank while convening a meeting, the notices containing the agenda items, supplementary notes sent before the mandatory notice period of Fourteen days to enable the Directors to go through them, jottings of the Directors views and questions for seeking clarifications at the meetings, the specific role of each Director in the different committees set up at the bank, record of various meetings attended by them, minutes recording discussions and critical resolutions passed, documented dissent, if any, towards any specific agenda point conveyed by some of the Directors, etc. The responses were all examined, recorded and assessed with a fine comb to establish without, a shred of doubt, the motives and direct or indirect involvement, if any, of the Chairman and members of the Board, in an effort to unearth the antecedents and the actors involved in the massive financial fraud.

4

THE ROLE OF THE CHAIRMAN AND THE BOARD TUMBLES OUT

It did not escape the Court's attention that often high value loans, running up to crores of rupees, were discussed and cleared by the Chairman within a short span of just one hour at board meetings that were specifically convened to discuss, deliberate and minute important discussions and decisions.

The court encouraged those Directors and Officials who wished to depose in camera for security reasons, to do so, by shifting the prosecution and defense attorneys to an adjacent enclosure away from the observers and press personnel.

Many startling facts were revealed in such closed door confessions. The court was shocked beyond words to know from the whistleblowers, the modus operandi and the high handed behaviour adopted by the Chairman. How the Chairman routinely used foul and un-parliamentary language to silence detractors, and drowned everyone's voice through high decibels. Though the Chairman boasted of high academic qualifications, when he opened his mouth during the meetings with the staff and board, he often used guttery language that could put any street side urchin to shame.

The Chairman demanded a standing ovation from the staff every time he made a grand entry at the office. The CEO and other officials were reduced to errand boys and hand maidens, carrying out odd jobs, including those of carrying the Chairman's briefcase, serving tea, standing in attendance, and opening the car door to usher the Chairman in and out. Often, in front of the Chairman's cronies, they even allowed themselves to be ridiculed and become the butt of jokes, expletives and unprintable language. The laughter such flowery language generated from those in the inner circle, would only sanction and embolden the Chairman to go on and on, unabated. In exchange for helping him derive such sadistic pleasure, the Chairman would look the other way with the CEO and other officials engaging in financial and non-financial aberrations, such as claiming cash reimbursement for travel and entertainment, attending personal work during office hours, owning multiple properties in different cities, much beyond their known source of income, etc.

In a way, it was turning out to be a convenient and cosy club, with each one encouraging the other to abuse power, in an atmosphere of bonhomie and in an attempt to justify each other's omissions and commissions. There was a tendency of each one scratching the back of the other to the detriment of the bank's and its depositor's interests. The Chairman was truly the master of everything that he surveyed. He had the reputation of hiring and firing officials at his whim and fancy and, often, through WhatsApp messages. As a result, key officials would dread opening WhatsApp messages, whenever they received messages from the Chairman on their mobile phones. No one at the bank had the guts to put up even a semblance of a fight with the Chairman, however justified he or she may be.

The court was apprised of the complete absence of transparency in dealings at the Head Office, and how the Chairman, although holding a non-executive position, insisted on being provided all the paraphernalia, including unheard of perks and made it a habit of attending office daily and interfering with the day to day operational matters at the bank, much against the comfort and liking of professional bankers and with utter disdain to RBI's stated policy on, governance and thereby, effectively created an alternate power structure at the bank.

The Bank's senior staff did not need much persuasion to sing like canaries before the Judges. In unison, the staff informed the bench that the Chairman and the Board would corner all praise if any good incident happened at the bank; however, if the external auditors or the Inspecting Officials pointed out any lapses or wrongdoings, they would conveniently feign ignorance and put on innocent faces, saying they were merely lending their name and time to the bank, despite their busy Schedules and that the day to day operations and crucial decisions were left to be taken by the CEO and top ranking officials possessing extensive banking experience.

At the meetings with the regulators, the Board would also have the audacity to point out that they were not aware of any such wrongful practices and that the CEO should have brought the same to their notice well in time for them to take remedial actions. However, the truth was that the Chairman and the Board were fully in the know of the lapses or non-compliance of norms and, most of the times, such decisions to cut corners and compromise with the norms would be taken at the behest and specific oral instructions of the Chairman.

The bank's team also informed the Court that many professional bankers had joined the bank to drive business and compliance, but left within a few months of joining, due to the high handed behaviour of the Chairman and Board. These bankers were hired with the promise that they would be the change agents and would receive complete support, freedom, and zero interference from the Board in the day to day operations of the bank. However, within a few days of joining, when these professional bankers were firmly in the saddle, the Chairman and the Board would start backseat driving and make veiled demands to the CEO to understand the culture of the bank and not ruffle feathers or disturb the equilibrium overnight, but to ensure that the status quo was maintained. All attempts were made surreptitiously for the CEO to continue with the culture at the bank, however much flawed and bereft it may be of the basic ethics and principle of fairness in banking.

In other words, the CEO would be asked to look the other way and put up with the many discrepancies and wrong practices being followed in the bank. The CEO would not even be permitted to pull up erring customers. If he ever crossed the line and asked the clients to comply with the Bank's norms or loan sanction terms, the Chairman would get to know of the same almost immediately and give a dressing down to the CEO for deciding to speak to the clients on his own, without consulting the Chairman or the Board. The CEO and high ranking experienced bankers were recruited after multiple interviews, by painting a rosy picture that the Board had decided to hire the candidate for his or her rich experience and that the Board would be open to giving him or her complete autonomy in implementing new ideas, best practices and processes. The reality, however, would be the exact opposite of what was promised at the interview.

When the candidate/s came on board, all their attempts to introduce new ideas and robust fraud-proof processes, would be fought tooth and nail by the very same Board, which, only a few days ago, had projected a holier than thou image of themselves. By this time, irreconcilable differences would have resulted, damaging the congenial working relationship between the CEO and the Board.

The pretence by the Chairman and the Board that they believed in adopting a professional hands-off approach in managing the bank, would hardly last for a few Board meetings. The CEO would soon come to experience the worst form of Corporate Governance standards. The mask would start peeling off, and the real face of the Chairman and Board would be revealed. However, by that time, it would be too late for the CEO to act, as they would have severed all relations with The previous employer and would have nowhere to go. They would then lick their wounds and suffer silently-disillusioned, defeated and cheated – to endure the uncouth behaviour of the Chairman and the Board, day in and day out. To the CEO and other high ranking officials, it was becoming clearer by the day that the Chairman and Board did not need the services of any professional banker, but just a yes man, more in the mould of their man Friday and a virtual rubber stamp.

The height of insult to the CEO and the other senior professional bankers would be the reaction of some of the Directors, who would generally remain silent in each meeting while discussing important agenda points. The only contribution from them would be nothing more than sipping tea, munching the wafers served at the meeting, and collecting their sitting fees. But on certain occasions, prompted by a vociferous nature of the Chairman, these Directors, notwithstanding their lack of knowledge in various finer aspects of banking, would get emboldened to raise certain innocuous and basic questions to the seasoned bankers. Just because they were part of the Board, they seemed to derive a divine right to ask any and every question, however silly it might be, to the professional bankers. At such times, all that the professional bankers could do was control their internal rage by managing a weak smile and mumble some incoherent response.

Clearly, the Chairman and the Board wanted a qualified and experienced banker at the helm of the affairs more as a decorative piece to showcase at various forums as a prized trophy and lend respectability to their Bank and the Board. Nonetheless, during the day to day working at the bank, the same professional banker would be required to eat a humble pie by being required to second all the questionable and murky dealings of the Chairman and the Board, with a mandate to give them a semblance of credibility.

In a few weeks, the CEO would be fully transformed. He would forget all that he had learnt in his life from some of the most professional banks, and before he could even realise, he would start singing to the tune of the Chairman and the Board, ensuring that the last wall of checks, balances and controls is made to collapse meekly, to the detriment of the bank's and its customer's interests.

Despite Corporate Governance and good practices becoming mandatory, the Chairman and the Board were locked in a time warp, suffering from an illusion that the practices being followed by them all these years were indeed time tested. Hence, the same could be continued, however faulty or out of step they be with the regulator's diktat and the winds of change blowing in the country.

The Board was also suffering from the fear of losing their importance in a transparent and professional environment. They, therefore, had to assert their importance through such high decibel orders to the CEO, which were clothed as requests or directions, but were nothing short of pressure on the professional bankers to cut corners, bend backwards or to look the other way while sanctioning fresh, high value loans and renewal of the existing ones, much against the remarks and explicit instructions of the credit, risk, audit and compliance teams.

The Board also had serious reservations on imbibing the email culture, and would always chide bankers whenever they insisted on documented instructions or recording detailed minutes of the meetings. The Board would constantly give confusing signals. While the members would keep forwarding messages showcasing best practices being followed in the industry and at other leading banks, when the same was suggested by the CEO and his colleagues at the Head office (HO), the Chairman and Board would take affront and withdraw into their shell. It was a case of wanting to see good practices and upright bankers in other banks, but continuing to be in denial or refuse to accept and acknowledge the fact that help was needed urgently at their own bank.

The Board would engage in a classic double speak by informing the seniors in the bank's HO not to concentrate only on community banking, as it is the stated objective of the Board to cater to the needs of different customer segments, in keeping with the mandate of the regulators. However, in practice, the Board would only encourage community banking by blindly considering unfeasible and below par loan proposals from the members of the community.

At times, the Board would show its keenness to embrace changes suggested by the regulator, but at the very next moment, it would go back to its original ways of disregarding dissenting voices and best practices. The bank was clearly becoming a victim of its own making and getting drawn deeper and deeper into an abyss. It was just a matter of time before the bank imploded.

The court was apprised on how the Chairman was not in the habit of giving instructions in writing or through emails, but would always shout instructions orally or over phone and follow them up for implementation. The court was also aghast to know that the Chairman and Board were in the habit of dismissing sound advice of professional bankers and using the senior bankers as a mere adjunct. The bank's coffers were used as petty cash by the Chairman and the Board. However, nothing was ever documented. They were wise and careful enough not to leave any traces.

No efforts were spared in abusing their power and earning extra income. The most common modus operandi would be to claim fuel reimbursements and food bills regularly. The voucher would be prepared by the bank's team and verified by the officer attached to the HO. The fuel and food bills would invariably be from a regular service provider or a restaurant. It was anybody's guess that these were merely accommodation bills. Similarly, inflated invoices for advertisements in unknown magazines would be cleared in a jiffy. Friends of the Chairman would be compensated for offering unheard of Marketing or Office Cleaning Services. The paper trail of such payments would be meticulously created, so as to avoid audit remarks. Known Charitable Institutions would be doled out donations at regular intervals for random events, with little or no co-relation to the bank's business.

Recruitment drives would be conducted regularly, and candidates paying the right price would be selected, despite their lack of talent or merit. Similarly, over-invoiced bills for giving a facelift to the static website of the bank or for the interior decoration of some of the branches, customer lobby, onsite ATM rooms or even the toilets, would be cleared. If this was not enough, an agency would be paid a hefty fee for building the brand of the bank, complete with an alternate logo and a glossy sign board of the bank and its branches.

No effort was spared to systematically milk the bank during the five year tenure of the Board. The vendors of all such services would be regulars on the panel of the bank. Details of such brash and brazen *quid pro quo* arrangements were getting strewn all over. The Bench was left speechless and was shaking its head in disbelief.

The Chairman's micro managing attitude was reducing the CEO and other top ranking officials to be mere onlookers, with the bank's machinery being used and abused to handle the Chairman's many personal duties. The Chairman had carefully cultivated sycophants and was vesting them with extra constitutional powers to create fear psychosis and an atmosphere of mistrust. These informers would report everything on a minute to minute basis to the Chairman.

The Court was apprised on how the less capable officers, owing complete loyalty and allegiance to the Chairman, were given special, out of turn increments and generous concessions, as well as insight into the ways in which the Registrar's and Employee Union's support was garnered through behind the scene manipulations.

That was not all. The Court was given finer details on how the Chairman was provided a furnished office room, where the prospective borrowers and agents would meet the Chairman holding court, often in isolation, without the involvement of any of the Management officials. The Chairman insisted that the closed circuit camera be removed from his chambers, so as to easily hatch conspiracies unrecorded, unseen and unheard by the rest in the bank, while, every other area of the bank had CCTV cameras installed as a standard operating procedure.

Also, the notice, agenda, board notes and minutes were all prepared to showcase the Chairman's version, with total disregard to the facts, norms and proceedings that actually transpired at such meetings. It was ensured that the agenda papers, running into hundreds of pages, were given to the other Directors merely twenty four hours before the meeting, so as to make sure that the Directors did not find enough time to go through important board notes or do their homework to be able to give their views meaningfully or ask the right questions at the meetings. The minutes were often prepared by the Chairman weeks and months after the respective meetings, just so that the other participants at such meetings could not even remember what was discussed and decided at such past meetings. The Chairman was indeed the emperor of everything that he surveyed and was nothing short of a judge, jury and executioner, all rolled into one, disregarding all voices of dissent and reason.

Further, high value loans were passed within minutes at these meetings, and valuable time at such meetings was wasted in discussing inconsequential administrative points. The employees not falling in line were transferred, or cajoled and coaxed into submission through false allegations, or slapped with cases requiring disciplinary action or bought by doling out of turn promotions, transfers to plum positions etc. The Chairman had different offers in his bag that no one seemed to refuse.

On certain occasions, the Chairman, Vice Chairman, and Directors would decide to descend on the branches of the bank, unannounced. At such times, as was customary, the Manager would vacate his seat and invite the Board Member to occupy it. This was his way for paying obeisance or respect and leaving the field wide open to the Board Member to meet and greet the customers, run the branch as he or she desired for the few hours or, at times, even for the entire day. The staff would be expected to stand in attendance, boosting the ego of the Board Member and also catering to every demand of the dignitary.

At such times, it would come as no surprise to the staff to notice that all the top borrowers of the branch would suddenly appear from nowhere, as if on a premonition, and would make a beeline to the cabin to hold an impromptu, closed door meeting. The Branch Manager would not be a part of such meetings, though he was heading the branch and responsible for the same. Instead, he would be made to run errands like arranging for water, tea, soft drinks, snacks, etc., for those holding court.

During such visits, the Board Member would also call up top officials at the HO from the branch where they would be camping. The borrowers would make many unreasonable demands, which the Board member would readily agree to and subsequently escalate in the strongest possible terms to the BM or the HOD at the HO. The tongue lashing that followed, would clearly convey who the Boss was. Any amount of explanation or logic would not work, and the borrower would be facilitated to ultimately have his way. If the GM or the CEO sought approvals for their actions through emails from the Board Member, he would give them a lesson in the culture of the bank and ridicule the seasoned bankers by pointing out that such an organised style of documenting every little thing might work well at a PSU or Private Bank, but not at the Co-Op Banks, where personal relationships count more than credit score, ratings, repayment capacity, financial discipline or any such compliance norms, documentation or paper work.

The revelations went on and on. How the risk department was asked to go easy and desist from giving strong comments on the loan proposals brought by the Chairman, whereas the very same risk department was at the behest of the chairman made to go the whole hog and pierce holes, without holding back any punches, on more meritorious loan proposals referred by other Directors. The Chairman made sure that the credit department used all the tools at its command to project, in a rosy manner, even the most unworthy loan proposals brought in by the Chairman, and in the process, deviate from established norms. However, the Chairman ensured that such sanction notes did not contain either his signature or his views leading to approval and the eventual sanction of the loans.

Loan proposals in which the Directors of a borrowing company faced legal, BIFR or NCLT cases, were considered favourably, by instructing the loan department officials to classify such stressed accounts as standard assets. Some of these accounts were ever-greened, thereby they would escape RBI filings.

Mandatory Provisions to be made against NPAs were not made adequately, ostensibly to increase the profits, thereby offering dividends to share-holders, in a bid to gain their loyalty and votes. A large sum of money would also get disbursed to the Chairman's preferred trusts as donations and subscriptions, to ensure victory at the elections, etc. Travel arrangements and ticketing would be invariably done through the firm where the Chairman or his family and friends had interests. Properties were also purchased in the name of known investors, in locations with very little business prospects, often at exorbitant rates, etc. The very same property would then get leased out to the bank on high lease rentals for long term tenure. All this was done in a brazen, nonchalant and devil may care attitude, to suggest that the Chairman was unaccountable and a law unto himself. There would be related party transactions galore. However, any incriminating remark made by the auditors would be shaken like water off a duck's back.

The height of misplaced priorities would be the steps taken to be in the good books of the political dispensation. The Chairman was known to contribute generously from the Bank's kitty to the various Relief Funds of the State, despite the Bank itself being in a precarious financial position. The group photographs taken during such public events would further be published in the local language newspapers as well as the Annual Report of the bank, showcasing the Board's initiatives towards Corporate Social Responsibility, made at the cost of the bank's and its depositor's interest. These exercises in Public Relations were largely made with a view to earn brownie points amongst members in the community. Thus, there seemed to be no one to question or seek accountability for the actions of the Fifteen wise men and women constituting the Board of the Bank.

The officials also were pained to explain how the Chairman and Board Members had a closed mind when it came to hearing about the ills affecting the bank and the many urgent steps that needed to be taken to arrest the rot. Saner voices and professional unbiased opinions were stifled, while sycophancy was expected, nurtured and suitably rewarded too.

The court was also informed that off late, the Chairman and the Board were waiting for their term to come to an end, as they felt the forthcoming scrutiny would be unbearable, and wanted to have a peaceful and unblemished exit. The heat in the kitchen was gradually increasing by the day. The Chairman and the entire Board knew that they were complicit in the loot and, hence, were trying their best to vamoose and jump off the sinking ship. Although, they had been in an illusory world of their own and given themselves the undeserved importance, yet they knew that their game was up. They were aware that a series of their wrongdoings would come to light sooner than later, and they may be ostracised for the same. They, therefore, wanted the baton to be passed on from them, to be carried by a new team, unaware of the murky dealings. Everyone from the Board was suddenly interested in relinquishing their position and seemed to be in an unusual hurry to get a safe passage.

The details spilled by the bank officials were exhaustive and left nothing to imagination. Such blatant and arrogant disregard in following basic norms to safeguard the hard earned money placed by common citizens was in complete contravention of banking rules and regulations. That such a violation had continued unabated for such a long time, made the court wonder how such misuse of power was possible despite several layers of checks and balances as well as compliance norms embedded in modern day banking.

For the court and its observers, the worst was yet to come.

While it was too early for the Bench to pass any judgement, they were unanimous in their observations. The head of the Bench, speaking for his colleagues, observed that accepting to shoulder the responsibility as a Director of a bank is no casual affair. Directors are required to understand the enormity of the responsibility cast on them. They are expected to read the Board notes carefully and put across their point of view on every agenda point, in an informed manner. Their views need to be properly captured through minutes and resolutions, for posterity. Ignorance is no excuse. The head of the Bench went on to explain that there were Doctors and professionals from non-accounting backgrounds who had lent their names and professional reputation to the Boards of banks and had agred to take on such a responsibility despite their busy schedule. Thought they may have remained absent for most of the meetings, they needed to explain to the court's satisfaction as to why they should be allowed to go scot free and not be made accountable for the bank's failure as the court held that they had fiduciary responsibility for ensuring the bank's well-being.

The court also educated the gathering that the Co-operative movement has become a success in various countries of the world, including India. Experiments such as Anand Milk Federation and the Agricultural produce co-operatives have been able to work in the true spirit of a Co-operation, by helping farmers with cold storage, distributing their produce, helping in value addition, getting appropriate prices and generally improving the lot of the people. Then, there are Co-operative Banks in Europe, who have gone public and even enjoy an AAA rating for their investment offerings.

The court in a candid manner observed that sadly, in our country, some of the Co-operative Banks seemed to have either forgotten or compromised the purpose for which they were formed. Instead of engaging in social banking to help the unbanked and under banked, these banks have permitted loss of their depositors savings and lost the trust of their customers who have been loyal to them for generations. The mismanagement in few of the banks has earned a bad name for the entire sector, which has had a cascading effect on other healthy banks too.

5

ONE MAN SHOW

It emerged that the Chairman had been virtually running the bank single-handedly and, thereby, enjoying immense authority sans any responsibility whatsoever, with utter disregard to all voices of dissent. High value loans to related parties continued to be given at the Chairman's behest, though such borrowers were defaulters elsewhere. In exchange for a share in the spoils, the CEO too was made a willing partner in all such decisions and sinister plans, by making use of his ingenuity to record transactions outside the Core Banking System of the bank and away from the glare of the outside world, so as to avoid any possible detection by the external auditors and RBI inspectors.

Though there was an Organization Chart and documented delegation of financial and non-financial powers, it was the Chairman who took all the decisions and was the *de facto* master of everything that he surveyed. No decision, whether small or big, would be taken or implemented without the Chairman's nod. Even during his absence, his omnipresence would invade each department and branch of the bank, overwhelming the staff and officers. Everyone was in a permanent state of intimidation. The over interference of the Chairman and the Board was to such an extent that, over the years, the CEO and other top ranking officials lost their confidence in taking even the smallest of decision without consulting the Chairman. It seemed that they had abdicated all powers, and taking decisions without crutches had altered their DNA permanently. The Chairman and the Board had completely hijacked and appropriated all the critical functions of the bank.

Though the Chairman would encourage the team to speak and come up with ideas, his mood would swing without much provocation, unexpectedly. During such times, the Chairman exhibited his worst temper tantrums and zero listening skills. Even though, at times the staff members, officers and directors would come up with brilliant ideas and practical suggestions in the best interest of the bank, if those ideas and suggestions were in variance or even differed slightly from the views of the Chairman, the officials would be given a tongue lashing and were shredded to pieces, never to ever stand up to give their opinion again. Such was the level of tyranny and refusal to consider voices of reason or counter views, that no one ever dared to open their mouth, except to meekly nod in agreement with every diktat of the Chairman.

The Chairman and the Board would give an impression that it is only they who have the interest of the bank at heart and a divine right to take all the decisions, often disregarding the sound advice given by the very professional bankers who were hired by the Board themselves, after an extensive interview process.

On occasions, when the CEO or the Head of Loans Department would refuse to consider a dodgy proposal favourably, the Chairman would fret and thunder that the proposal needed to be considered and an appropriately worded note should be placed, recommending such a proposal for the Board to undertake collective deliberations and decision making. Though there was a semblance of a committee approach, for all practical purposes it was a one man show, with the Chairman driving the discussions and decisions at the Board meeting.

If the CEO and the top professional bankers persisted with their views not to consider a loan proposal as it lacked merit or had too many deviations and irregularities, the Chairman would laugh and wink at the other Directors, saying that is the very reason we hired professional bankers, isn't it? It was the job of the CEO and the Loans Department to make sure that such proposals were doable and they were expected to put on their thinking caps and make things happen without citing any excuses and/or Pointing out any present or potential risks.

It was amply clear at such meetings as to who the boss was. The CEO was reduced to a toothless paper tiger with a high salary and perks to go with the designation, which was inherently a sinecure position. Even when a staff had to be counselled or disciplined for insubordination, the staff would know which strings to pull and who to contact to tilt the cart against the CEO. Within minutes of the CEO taking a decision in the interest of the bank, he would promptly get a call from the extra constitutional powers to reinstate the errant staff with full honours, as the staff member was a right hand man of the Chairman or one of the Board members. Such staff would be pampered due to their abilities to mobilise maximum votes from the share-holders for the Chairman and his team during the elections, for a repeat term. Allegiance and loyalty to the Chairman and the Board, and not to the institution, was what mattered the most.

The CEO and professional bankers would soon learn to give up and respect the wheels within wheels, the informal reporting lines, and the conspicuous power centre. It was made abundantly clear that if the CEO and the professional bankers in the bank need to maintain peace and harmony at the bank, they should learn to look the other way and not to ever ruffle feathers of the powers or take unpleasant decisions.

All these incriminating facts were being spilled out by the officials at the tell-all, closed door depositions. It was getting clearer that an organised crime was being committed day in and day out in the name of banking, without firing a single shot or spilling any blood. The parallel center of power was extremely active and it was they who were running the bank, systematically emptying the coffers by fudging the bank's books for accommodating high value transactions to a syndicate of corporate customers. These acts were done at the behest and with the knowledge, connivance and consent of the Chairman and some of the Board Members, along with the active participation of the CEO and high ranking officials.

Thousands of marked dormant and inactive accounts were activated to route low value book entries below a certain threshold level so as to escape detection, all in the hope that when repayment came through in the future from the related parties, the reversal entries would be passed to the maze of accounts, erasing all trails. Thus, the violations would eventually get covered without leaving any trace of the same. The fraud structured through a series of financial accommodation entries to the known clients were for a short or medium term. The money of the unsuspecting depositors were being used to fund these nefarious transactions, all in the hope that the funds would get repaid and the temporary aberration would get corrected eventually and thereby ensuring that all is well that ends well. However, such happy endings were fraught with huge operational, credit, and market risks, which none of the players were aware of or prepared to acknowledge in their greed to make a fast buck.

Every effort was made by the Chairman to buy the loyalty and silence of the Directors by various means. Despite the bank not posting respectable profits, the sitting fees for the Directors attending the various meetings would be increased manifold by the Chairman, thereby making every Director party to the loot. Although the Directors would often attend multiple meetings on the same day, their sitting fee would get paid out separately for each meeting.

The party went on unabated at the cost of the bank and no one was complaining. Double standards were practiced and legitimate demands of the staff, such as permitting encashment of un-availed leaves or payment of minimum bonus, were not heeded, citing the bank's precarious health.

The various personal businesses of the Directors, related party transactions with the bank, their own deposits and those of their family members' held with the bank, its value, mandatory disclosures that they had to make to the regulator as well as links with the Corporate Borrowers, which turned into quick mortality/Non Performing Assets, were all brought up one by one and documented in court. Every decision taken since the time the board was first elected and later re-elected after the initial five year term was dissected to establish unholy alliances, if any, and mala fide considerations.

Carton loads of documents, including vendor agreements, donations and subscriptions to various Trusts and Charities run by the Directors directly or through proxy, etc. were examined, admitted and taken into the court's custody as critical evidence in support of the many arguments.

The court was getting convinced that the Chairman was a crafty, master manipulator, investing all his time and energy to play on all sides, and keep everyone happy, to ensure no one raised a finger. A loyal set of share-holders were also being carefully cultivated to assure multiple terms for the board. A visionary, no doubt, but having such misplaced priorities that he would use all his talent and skills to strip the bank of its funds and cause grave injury to the sound health of the bank. In some circles, the Chairman had come to be called as the 5% authority.

During one of the appearances, when a member of the Bench innocently asked the Chairman to explain the power structure at the Bank, the Chairman, in what could be termed as a Freudian slip of tongue, countered saying there is only one power center at the bank and that he is the Power

Center as the Chairman of the bank. The observers gathered in court could not believe what they had just heard. Coming from the voluntary admission made by the Chairman, it was the final nail in the coffin. No amount of future clarification made would enable him to extricate himself from what he had just admitted to in full consciousness and in the presence of the entire court.

6

THE WILLING CEO

Later, the same process of examination was followed with the CEO and Heads of Department as well as with all those officials who had enjoyed delegated financial and non-financial decision making powers. Their role in the abetment to the crime, suspected *quid pro quo*, link with the various vendors, trusts and associations, their known names, aliases, wives, girl-friends, paramours were all traced and summoned to depose.

The chain of letters, emails and WhatsApp messages sent by the CEO to the customers in an effort to reassure them before the scam eventually spun out of the CEO's control, blowing on the face of the depositors, were documented to trace the series of well thought out misrepresentations, lies and breach of trust.

To be fair to the CEO, it was getting clearer that he was qualified and capable of functioning on his own and, from the documented minutes of the initial years, it could be seen that he did show his acumen as well as voice his dissent now and then. His arguments and reasoning, however, were invariably getting drowned in the din. That is when he felt that instead of exhausting his lung power at every meeting, it was a better option, under the circumstances, to cross over to the other camp by shaking hands with the Chairman and the Board and play ball to be in their good books. The court deduced the gradual transformation of the CEO from all the documented board notes, the various noting, minutes, resolutions and back papers of the various large loans, which eventually turned bad and into non-performing caustic assets.

Being an old timer at the Bank, the CEO had complete knowledge of all the mis-deeds and steps that needed to be taken to cover their tracks. The CEO was, in effect, facilitating smooth and perpetual loot at the bank, by designing fool-proof internal processes to give legitimacy to the transactions.

Personal assets of the bank officials were also valued vis-à-vis their known source of income. Discrepancies were flagged off, justifications sought, and responses recorded. Bank statements, title deeds of movable and immovable properties, as well as their personal effects, were thoroughly examined. Assets in the name of spouse, son, daughter, son-in-law, daughter-in-law and all those who are included under the definition of family, were included in the search. Those who were known to have illicit relationships were subjected to enhanced due diligence, covering even non-family members. The net was getting wider by the day.

Specific reasons for all the high value withdrawals, amounting to crores of rupees, made by some known insiders and entities, just days before the scam broke and restrictions on withdrawals imposed, through bearer cheques or via cheques presented in Cheque Truncation Clearing, vide electronic funds transfer modes such as Real Time Gross Settlement (RTGS), National Electronic Funds Transfer (NEFT), Immediate Payment System (IMPS), cross border transfers in various currencies vide Society for World-wide Inter-bank Financial Telecommunication (SWIFT), copies of the Message Transmission reports, the value date of such transactions, the beneficiary (BEN) details, Nostro Account statement of the bank with its overseas correspondent banks, Bills Discounted in Indian Rupees with the banks of the counter parties vide RBI's dedicated SFMS (Structured Financial Messaging System) Inter-bank platform, etc., were verified to assess the exact value of such withdrawals and transactions that were made just days before the bank's management decided to come clean with the RBI.

The Court was systematically going through a mountain of evidence, courtesy the banking interlocutors specifically appointed to help the Court in mapping the money trail from the failed bank to different beneficiaries. Obviously, some of these hurried transactions could not have occurred without such customers being privy to or getting to know about the bank's imminent collapse. There was no doubt that there were moles within the Bank's management or the Board, facilitating such last minute flight of funds by their near and dear ones from the soon to be defunct bank.

It was a case of the horse being allowed to conveniently gallop away, making all superfluous attempts thereafter to bolt the stable doors. All the details were painstakingly noted and recorded.

The bank's exposure in the Treasury business vide investments with other banks, T-Bills, Government Securities, Mutual Funds, Corporate Deposits, their investment grade ratings, etc., were also collated.

Structured loans, Dealership financing, arrangement with the Business Facilitators and Business Correspondents, breach of single party and group exposure norms through a maze of clever structuring of such loans, syndicated and consortium loans, etc., were all examined one by one. Also, the list of properties purchased for the bank's branches, their agreement values, fair values, ready reckoner values, etc., were noted to arrive at any attempt made towards over-invoicing.

Any intangible/exotic collateral securities provided by the Corporate borrowers for securing high value loans by offering their goodwill or brand value, high speed fleet of cars, yachts, private jets, corporate guarantees of shell companies and various attempts at layering, were all examined.

Clearly, the court was not taking chances with any possible escape or leakage of information, but was taking all the necessary steps required to plug the holes and arrive at correct assessments of *bona fide* utilisation of the bank's funds, by ring fencing those transactions having justifications, legitimate vouchers and transaction trails backed by legitimate underlying assets.

Efforts were systematically made by the Court to arrive at the near exact figure of funds lost or laundered and those where the securities were held, having a fair chance of recovery at a most conservative market value.

7

THE GREAT COMPROMISING ACT

The reports of the internal auditors, concurrent auditors, statutory auditors, yearly RBI audit reports, the minutes of the audit committee meetings, the red flags, dissents of Directors, if any, and reasons for its continuing non-compliance, were all brought up, discussed and inferences drawn. Reasons for not highlighting defaults in serving interest and for non-repayment of principle in high value accounts well in time were also sought. Similarly, the rationale for not renewing facilities well beyond their due date and failing to classify such accounts as sub-standard or NPA was also demanded and responses recorded. Clearly, the Court was being advised by a set of hardcore bankers on where exactly to look for anomalies.

The bank's correct financial position, based on the forensic audit done at the behest of the RBI, post the appointment of the administrator, was also examined and tallied with the bank's statements filed periodically with the RBI. Mismatches in the same were taken note of and explanations sought from the respective officials.

Internal processes and policies such as Credit Policy, Investment Policy, Audit Policy, IT Policy, Credit, Operational and Market Risk Policy as well as Risk Categorisation of Accounts and HR Policy adopted by the bank, were all assessed to establish the prevalence of best practices and conspicuous gaps, if any, at the bank. The process flow adopted to apprise any new high value loan proposal and for the renewal of existing loan facility of large corporate customers was also examined.

Heads of the Credit and Audit Departments, Committee of Executives sanctioning high value loans, Risk Department, and the risk notes accompanying large value loans were called for and examined with specific reference to the subsequent fall-out and increase in non-performing loans. Sanction terms, conditions precedent, conditions subsequent to disbursement, compliance thereof, role of outside agencies, their qualifications and criteria for appointment in the bank's panel for conducting search and valuation of collateral security and for creation of charge on the same in the bank's name, gaping holes, if any, were also pin pointed.

Reasons for repeated non-compliance of the Audit remarks in high value loans were questioned, and the internal and external auditors were pulled up for giving a clean chit and certificate to the bank's team despite such non-compliance of crucial norms. Very clearly, the audit team had failed to perform their role of being the watchdog and guiding the bank well in advance. Even their remarks were worded in a soft language, thereby giving an impression that they were merely going with the motion in a casual and diplomatic manner to avoid hurting the sentiments of the Board. For such a soft approach, their audit fees were commensurately enhanced regularly without any negotiations.

The court was scrutinising every nook and corner, and skeletons started piling up.

REGULATOR BLINKS AND TRIES TO PASS THE BUCK

In-depth cross examination was reserved for the Inspecting Officials from the RBI and the team from the Registrar's Office, that had visited the bank during the past decade and conducted its audit and inspection.

Reasons behind the RBI granting an A rating, and justifications for granting the status of being a Financially Sound and Well Managed (FSWM) bank, were thoroughly examined and justification was sought from the respective officers for their actions. Similarly, the Registrar's, action or lack of it, despite the RBI flagging off certain glaring irregularities and Recommending the suspension of Chairman and MD, were also examined. Answers for inaction or lack of follow up for finding solutions towards a logical end were sought from both the regulators, and the same was recorded.

Frequent mention and observations, year after year, of the same irregularities, such as holding large number of transactions in the excel format outside the Core Banking System of the bank, reasons for non-compliance, and regulator's lack of justification to flag them off as a major deviation, instead merely remarking them as a minor non-compliance, were all recorded. While the inspectors were found to be doing their job dispassionately, it was clearly emerging that they had left much to be covered in terms of its completeness and in taking the inspection to its logical conclusion.

The court also observed that while the regulator had recommended, post its inspection of the Bank, certain dos and don'ts and corrective steps to be taken by the Registrar, there was no follow up and action taken report sought by the regulator. The regulators were seen to be doing their job without seeking a final closure on some of the key damning observations thus, reducing its exercise to a mere formality and, in the process, willy-nilly being a party in misguiding the depositors with an implied assurance that their deposits were safe, as the bank was given an A rating and the status of a FSWM bank. All this led to the regulators losing sheen and a dent in their reputation in the court of public opinion and common perception, even as the Bench was yet to pass its judgement. No amount of reasoning or justification could extricate the regulators from what seemed to be their failure and being found to be allegedly complicit in the mountain of unintentional commission and omission leading up to the collapse of the bank.

The regulator team was also seen to be in great pain to explain to the court that although some of the smaller banks had a good team and the financial capability to imbibe and implement best practices, there existed an unfounded fear in the minds of the Chairman and amongst the Board Members at some of the larger banks of losing their control and importance if their banks were to adopt a more professional working style.

The regulator went on to opine that while in public and in their interactions with the regulator during the yearly Annual General Meeting of the share-holders as well as at the internal meetings with the staff of the bank, the Board seemed to profess a transparent and professional approach, in private, they lacked the will to change or engage in participative management or let go of their strangle hold on the bank and practice a hands-off approach. The Board did not show the will to change or bite the bullet, and embrace change when it was needed the most. Though the Board saw the writing on the wall that their end game was nearing, it was common knowledge in the bank that the Board fought shy of articulating their stand and exhibited a tremendous resistance to change.

The Boards at some of the banks seemed to abhor being regulated or told how to run their bank and become regulatory compliant. They felt it is their divine right to run the bank as they had been doing in the past. Even though the opinion filed by the regulators was true, it was also seen to be an attempt to smartly pass the buck and get a clean chit themselves.

9

THE MUCK RUNS DEEPER

The court was unearthing plenty of anomalies and the casual nature of working adopted by all the stakeholders within and outside the bank. It was leading to a certain clash of interest situation, thereby resulting in connivance and compromise between the checks and balances of the system, which are crucial for ensuring the health of the bank and for the smooth running of its functions.

What started off as a case of financial mismanagement and fraud, was fast emerging to be the tip of the proverbial iceberg. The Court was questioning the ethics, morals, and the very foundation of propriety, moral turpitude and personal misdemeanour of those in the high seats of power and responsibility, whose actions were sure to have a damning impact on the interests of the bank's customers. The court observed in the passing, much to the amusement of everyone present, that with so many alleged short comings, it was surprising how the bank managed to function without any major hiccup for so long and that an accident of this magnitude, which was only waiting to happen sooner or later, had indeed got delayed due to some inexplicable reason, which was nothing short of a miracle through unexplained, divine intervention.

To the Bench, it was becoming a financial maze with too much data to comprehend. They had to listen with rapt attention and understand the proceedings without being tempted to pre-judge any of the accused. They had to rely not only on the arguments placed before them, but more importantly, on the several documentary evidences presented in support of those arguments. To some, it was proving to be difficult to decode and decipher many of the financial terms, models and internal processes adopted at the bank. So, they had to very frequently summon the court appointed panel of bankers with domain knowledge expertise, to clarify and demystify some of the intricate processes proceedings and financial terminology.

10

MEDIA KEEPS UP THE MOMENTUM

With the case generating daily updates in the print media and still trending on the electronic media even after nearly one full year since it was first detected, the interest in the case refused to die down.

Most of the daily newspapers carried an exclusive column, and news channels dedicated slots during prime time to provide updates on the case. Debates on the role and responsibility of the bank's management, auditors and regulators, and governance standards at the banks, the toll it had taken on many of its depositors, including deaths of as many as 60 innocent depositors, etc., was becoming fodder for both the print and electronic media. The purists in the banking and finance field argued an immediate need to have a single regulator for all those entities that were mobilising deposits from the common people. These academicians felt that dual authority and lack of regulatory clarity was allowing such major frauds escape from getting detected well in time and action getting initiated. Lessons needed to be learnt without any more lapse in time.

The domino effect was witnessed at many other banks, with depositors lining up and giving different excuses to pull out their funds from similar banks. Once considered a safe place to park their funds, the average customer was getting increasingly paranoid and disillusioned about banks. The trust quotient for banks was at an all-time low. The very same customers who had taken to banking and embraced digital banking were now seen to be holding large liquid cash in their homes. The customers did not have sufficient knowledge on which bank to invest in or get any satisfactory reassurances not to equate other banks with the one that had gone rogue. A concerted effort was quickly required to educate the depositors and allay their fears if the very foundation of banking was to be protected.

The court had the humongous task of rummaging through piles of information and making sense of it. On the road, the woes of the depositors continued unabated. Dreams were getting shattered, personal relationships were turning sour, self-respecting citizens were reduced to penury and were required to borrow from friends and relatives to stay alive, credit histories of honest tax payers and those who never missed on repaying a loan instalment in their life were getting affected beyond repair. The financial tsunami of the scam had spared no one in its wake, without slowing or showing any discrimination towards its victims based on the class, gender, religion, literacy levels or economic strata of society that they belonged to.

11

DAMAGE CONTROL – TOO LITTLE, TOO LATE

The damage and excruciating pain inflicted by the failure of a large bank had spared no one. Both the customers and the regulators seemed to be equally foxed and lacked the reflexes to deal with the after effects of the mammoth fraud as it unfolded.

On a lighter note, one of the popular jokes doing the rounds was that the regulator would indeed find a way to bail out the failed bank, as hundreds of high ranking employees of the regulator themselves had invested, through their Credit Society, funds amounting to over a Hundred Crores of Rupees in the failed bank. This reason may well act as the single most saving grace in an otherwise seemingly hopeless situation and serve as the impetus to find an amicable solution soon.

Those who had less than INR 100,000 with the bank, got their savings back after spending a few anxious months. However, for those who were unfortunate to park their funds in excess of the threshold in the bank that went rogue, there was no immediate solution in sight.

No effort was spared by the customers, who, thanks to the social media, would group and rally around each other often at a short notice at various pockets in the city, near the branches of the bank, in front of the regulator's office, opposite a politician's bungalow, at the city's various large parks, busy traffic intersections, places of worship and also through posts in different WhatsApp groups, twitter handles, mid-night candle light vigils, etc. They also mildly threatened boycotting the state elections and met the Governor, Finance Minister and even the Leader of the Opposition to drum up support from the high and mighty across the political divide.

Although those holding high offices gave the depositors a sympathetic hearing and tried to assuage their hardship through consolatory words and many comforting statements, they fell awfully short of any concrete solution to bring closure to the woes of thousands, and were thus reduced to being a mere lip service and hollow assurance to resolve the no-win situation.

No one had a ready fix solution to the financial mess left by the bank in the lives of thousands of its depositors. Meanwhile, every day brought in fresh revelations; How large loans were sanctioned at less than half the collateral security to the loan ratio, without following the due process, how the end use of such loans was not monitored, leaving the borrower to merrily divert the funds to buy property in the country and abroad as well as indulge in an obscene show of wealth, albeit borrowed ones, to buy fancy cars, jets, yachts, gold and diamond ornaments and enjoy a lavish lifestyle by siphoning off the bank's funds.

How family members and, in some cases, even their drivers and gardeners, were employed or inducted as dummy directors to the Board of their Companies, to hold high offices with ceremonial designations, to swindle and launder large sums of money through unimaginable pay packages and perks. How even an ex-regulator, now a high ranking officer in the payroll of the bank, had compromised and charmed his way to conceal the serious anomalies from the prying eyes of the inspecting officials visiting the bank year after year. There were allegations that the officer had played an active role in mobilising high value funds of the employees' credit society of the regulator. He obviously seemed to know his way around and was only too familiar with the way the trustees worked at the credit society and how they could be impressed upon to park high value funds with the bank.

The last straw on the back of the depositors was the measure announced in the finance bill for the forthcoming year. Thanks to the bank sinking under its weight of non-performing assets, the bill came up with a proposal to re-calibrate the insurance cover on the bank deposits, through a realistic five-fold increase, in an attempt to make the same more relevant to the needs of the present times as well as safe guard the interests of depositors of all such bleeding banks in the future. Although the bill was well received, being prospective, it did not offer any immediate relief to the depositors of the beleaguered bank, which had gobbled up the deposits of its trusting customers. However, the effect and shortcomings of such well-meaning measures were not wholly unexpected in the informed circles.

The failure of the bank, its massive impact on the depositors and the inability of the regulator to find an amicable solution, even after the lapse of 1 year from the date of the bank's collapse, compelled the initiation of several far reaching regulatory reforms. These included placing a temporary freeze on dividend pay outs of the shares held by members of such shadow banks as well as a temporary embargo on the refund of the face value of the shares, thereby putting many shareholders of these banks, across the country, into huge misery.

While the measures, understandably, were taken to stem the rot, ramp up the reserves, and protect the share capital from getting eroded, such steps were open to being challenged in the legal circles, as the shares in the first place, were subscribed by borrowers as a part of the mandatory loan sanction terms. It was compulsory for them to do so as a part of the contractual loan approval process. Therefore, by the same token, it was implied that their shares subscription would be available for refund once their loans were repaid in full. This was the prevalent practice in the sector, as such shares issued by the shadow banks to its members were neither assignable nor tradable in the market. The only option was to surrender the shares to the issuer of the same. In this context, however compelling the reasons may be for not refunding the share capital, especially to such borrowers who do not have any dues or financial liability to the banks, this step was being perceived as a restrictive practice to say the least. It was to further go on to add to the trust deficit already prevailing in the sector due to the recent events.

While everyone wished the depositors to get tangible financial help, with banks of different sizes and shapes going belly up with unfailing regularity, it seemed unrealistic to expect the government to offer a financial package to bailout a bank, lest it become a norm and set a precedent for the government to do so in every future case to solve the misdemeanour of an unscrupulous bank. There appeared to be many banks in various stages of financial decay and imminent collapse, needing immediate help. Any largesse in the form of a financial bailout was expected to open up many a Pandora's box.

With the entire sector gaining criticism from all quarters, it was getting difficult to attract new talent. The peculiar, interfering and unprofessional working style had disillusioned many an eminent banker from associating with the sector, dubbing it as a lost cause. The many skeletons emerging from the closet of the banks did not help their image any better.

The court felt compelled to opine that it is true that in a country where the people get a government they deserve, so too in the world of finance, so long as the depositors do not exercise caution or be vigilant, there will always be the fly by night operators, the emboldened Ponzi scheme scamsters, the multi-level marketers, the grave diggers and email phishers wanting to bequeath the fortune of a wealthy widow for a small handling charge, the con artists from villages like Jamtara, wanting to send their victims on a holiday of a lifetime, and the unscrupulous bankers who would wipe out the life savings of customers with a straight face. All of them will find it easier to continue with their modus operandi as long as there are naïve depositors who do not take even the basic steps to check the veracity and health of the bank where they park their funds.

Governments cannot be held accountable for the error in judgement or casual attitude of the people. Ignorance is often not a valid excuse under law. Basic due diligence and vigilance is expected from everyone so that they do not end up repenting at leisure.

It is expected of the depositors to take certain basic steps to stay safe in a world where ethics and principles are at an all-time low, in most walks of life. Banking is just a reflection of the times we live in. It is, therefore, the responsibility of every one to be more careful, vigilant and prudent, so that they do not keep encouraging scamsters to continue with their fraudulend expeditions.

SAMPLE OF FRAUDULENT LOAN CASES

The court was shocked and amused, in turns, with the information shared by the bank officials. It clearly showed the ingenuity with which the fraud was committed at their bank, as well as some of the frauds that were committed in general across various banks.

The bankers informed the court that the staff at the branches worked like the proverbial busy bee, collecting small and large deposits from the household and other customer segments in the vicinity of their branches. These deposits were the lifeline of the banks, the raw material and the very fuel for the banks to lend, invest and earn good returns on its loans and investments, to pay for the salaries, meet overheads, pay interest on the deposits and also to earn a reasonable profit. This would then be shared, post operational expenses and taxes, as dividend to its shareholders, contribute to the various reserve funds and, finally, towards the bonus and increment in salaries for the employees of the bank.

The bankers went on and on with their tutorial to those gathered in the court. They explained that garnering deposits needed persuasive skills and good customer service levels as well as competitive interest rates. However, in general, it was not a challenge or difficult to acquire and retain deposits.

Nonetheless, it is the loan portfolio which brought in the income for the bank and it was these loans – small and large – which were fraught with risks and had the capacity to endanger the bank. Hence, sanctioning loans needed a very high degree of analytical and assessment skills as well as a heightened degree of monitoring mechanism and predictive analysis.

The Court was then served a wide variety of case studies of different frauds to highlight the ingenuity of the fraudsters. Some of such cases were:

In a case straight out of the movies, a term loan was availed by a company, through the recommendation of the Chairman, for prawn cultivation. The loan, running into few Crores of Rupees, turned out to be a case of quick mortality. On investigation, it was found that the borrower was a shell company. The loan was traced to the Chairman, the ultimate beneficial owner. The papers given as security turned out to be that of a land taken on long lease, with very little chance of the money ever coming back.

In another case, a Director went out of his way to help the bank increase its loan portfolio. A customer holding a National Savings Certificate of nearly a crore of Rupees was accorded a loan of 75% of the face value of the NSC, without observing the standard operating procedure of getting the NSC lien marked with the issuing post office before disbursal of the loan. During the *post facto* audit check, it turned out that the NSCs were colour photo copies and on further field visit to the issuing post office, it was discovered that such a post office did not exist in the first place. The loan disbursed by the bank went up in smoke.

A third case was that of an enhancement application for an existing mortgage loan. Just before the loan was granted, a visit to the property revealed that the property had been razed to the ground many months back and that the reconstruction project was stalled, thereby jeopardising the bank's existing mortgage loan disbursed on the property. There was no question of giving any enhancement.

Then, there were umpteen number of cases found, wherein the loan to value ratio of the security was heavily compromised. Enhancing the value of the security to get higher loan amounts was the commonest of the no brainer ploys adopted to defraud banks.

Similarly, cases of ever-greening were identified, wherein loans long overdue were closed at one branch and the same were sanctioned as fresh loans at another branch of the bank, giving the borrower further breathing time to set right the fresh loan.

In another case of brazenness, a high value loan was granted to a manufacturing unit, merely on the basis of book debts and stock. On an inspection visit to the unit, it was brought to light that the unit had stopped operating many months back and that the workers on their muster were temporary labourers. The electricity bill of the unit, which was stated to be running in three shifts, was hardly few hundred rupees per month. The machines had gathered dust and the tea vendor in the vicinity complained that his tea bills of a thousand rupees were outstanding for the past few months. A loan, if sanctioned to the borrower, would have surely been diverted from the stated purpose and resultantly become an NPA within days.

Then, there was a case where on the strength of the Chairman's reference, a proposal for maximum permissible loan as per exposure norms was being considered, for putting up a solar power plant in another state, with unrealistically high projections of future receivables. On closer examination, it was found that the tariffs of solar energy had been over projected. In reality, the tariff had come crashing down lately and the project, based on its future receivables, was unviable. On rejection of the proposal, the client turned innovative to come up with a proposal for a similar value, this time for the renovation of a hotel resort in another state beyond the bank's jurisdiction. It was clearly a case prompting the bank to stay away from such proposals in which it had very limited appraisal skills. As it emerged later, the proposals were actively solicited by the Chairman, knowing fully well that the project was beyond the bank's jurisdiction. The Chairman wanted his known party to get the bank's loan by hook or by crook.

Yet another Director helped the bank to mobilise a large number of small loans from teachers. After a few months, when the loans started turning bad one by one, it was found that the teachers were all Benami and their names were nowhere to be found in the attendance registers of the institutions. If only an in-depth pre-sanction investigation had been carried out, this fraud could have been avoided.

There was another case where many large loans were granted through agents. When the loans became stressed, it was clear that the grant of the loans could not have been possible without the connivance of the bank officials.

A case was presented, wherein the Chairman introduced a Direct Selling Agency offering a portfolio of a large number of MSME loans at terms which were clearly one sided. The agency earned heavy upfront fees on each loan, without taking responsibility for collection or recovery. No surprise, the loans went bad and the bank was left holding the junk loans.

There were regular cases of multiple banks giving loans on common security, without the knowledge of other banks disbursing loans to the same borrower on the same security. Again, one of the oldest ploys in the book to defraud banks.

Similarly, there were banks saddled with loans, where the properties that were given as original collateral were replaced with collaterals of lesser market value and lower potential of getting disposed in times of default when the bank wished to sell it to recover its loans. Clever borrowers would try to palm of such ill liquid assets to unsuspecting banks with the help of the accommodating Management and Board.

There were a number of loans given to parties by discounting suspect accommodation bills under a structured financial messaging system, without underlying genuine trade transactions.

To accommodate known borrowers, mortgage loans were taken over and booked as home loans, giving the benefit of concessional home loan rates and other tax sops.

The Court was also apprised of genuine cases, wherein sanctioned loan amounts were lesser than the requirement made by the borrowers to run their business efficiently. Such loans eventually went bad, as the bank showed little or no sensitivity or imagination to handhold such borrowers through appropriate loan appraisal skills.

Purchase of premises for branches or godowns were made at the behest of the Chairman, often at exorbitant rates when compared to the prevailing rates in the area.

Arrangements were reached with Dealers of vehicles, wherein the loan amount was funded to the Dealer and from there to its in-house NBFC for disbursement of loans at higher interest rates to the same set of borrowers. The Dealer and NBFC, thus made a killing by way of piggy back riding on the bank's funds, taken at a competitive pricing. To top it, the vehicles for which the loans were granted, were to be mortgaged to the bank, but were mortgaged instead to the NBFC. It was only a matter of time before the entire loan would go bad and non-performing.

Board Members indulged in identifying and sanctioning loans through designated branches to small traders without following prudential norms for the same. When the loan went bad, sooner or later, the unfortunate Branch Manager would then be pressurised to undertake an extensive time consuming recovery process. In the event The branch manager failed he would be dubbed as being ineffective or good for nothing.

The Court inferred that these sample cases were merely few representational ones and that if the surface of the banks were to be scratched further, many such cases would emerge. The Court in its wisdom was constrained to observe that the value of the NPAs was in direct proportion to the single party and group exposure norms of various banks. Suffice to say, the bane of the NPA had not spared any bank and was plaguing banks of all sizes and shapes, resulting into the slow death of these institutions.

The Court came to an interim conclusion that however much policing is done, a percentage of Fraud and NPA were inherent in any bank. Such instances, however, are isolated and do not pull a bank down except for burning a small hole in the Balance Sheet. However, when the Board and Top Management themselves stoop down to abusing their power and are in cahoots to loot the bank systematically by throwing all checks and controls to the wind, under such circumstances, the fall of the bank, sooner or later, is a certainty.

SECTION 02

The Tales of Human Tragedy, Each Different from the Other Yet Inextricably Interwoven

01

A MARRIAGE STOPS

Alka, the only daughter of the Khuranas, was studious, a class topper all through, and yet, down to earth. She was known in Khalsa College as much for being a merit holder year after year as for her stunning looks. She was not just all brains, but an athlete and excellent debater too.

Although simple in her attire and lifestyle, she was endowed with a rare, sublime beauty that she carried with great dignity. This made her an instant favourite amongst everyone in college, more particularly with the senior boys, who clamoured for her attention, and desired to take her on a date. She, being focused on academics, was successful in warding off everyone's advances and had migrated to Manchester four years ago, in order to pursue her ambition of making a mark in her chosen field of psychiatry and making her parents proud.

For the past five decades, her family had been living in a pre-dominantly middle-income neighbourhood of Sion Koliwada. They were known for their honesty, friendly behaviour, and the hard work of 16-hours per day of the week that Khurana was putting into his small automobile accessories shop.

That day, Alka was returning home for an extended holiday of eight weeks to be with her parents and friends. She had also finally given a nod to her parents to fix her marriage with Daljeet, an IT professional and the son of a distant relative. Just like her, Daljeet too was meritorious in academics and had a passion for travel. He could manage to get an in-principle approval from his company for a transfer to the UK after his wedding to Alka. He was all set to settle down with her in London.

The Khuranas were looking forward to celebrating the marriage of their daughter with great pomp and show. They had meticulously planned the list of invitees, their stay arrangements, travel, food, presents, and giveaways. Indeed, the Khuranas had done well for themselves, and they were convinced that there was nothing that could stop them from carrying out the most important responsibility of their life, within just a few days. They had saved enough with their preferred local bank for the celebrations in the family, that was scheduled to happen within a few days. There was no stopping them, having come so far. But providence had other plans……

02

HOME BUSINESS GETS KILLED BEFORE IT STARTS

In another part of the city, within Asia's biggest slum, a story of grit and hope was Playing out.

Murugan and his wife Selvi, hailed from Theni, a small village on the outskirts of Madurai. Both of them got married young, as was customary in their community. After doing odd jobs in a beedi rolling home business run by the local village head, Murugan was bitten by the bug to get out of Theni and do something serious with his life. In this, he had his wife Selvi's complete support as she trusted her husband's capabilities immensely.

Murugan had long heard of Dharavi in Mumbai, and how those like him who migrated from Madurai, Thirunelvelli, and other parts of Tamil Nadu, had been prospering there due to their sheer hard work and entrepreneurial attitude. He had visited Dharavi twice as a part of his recce and was convinced that Dharavi was indeed the road to achieving glory.

With wife Selvi in tow and few of his possessions, Murugan had migrated to Dharavi some ten years ago. After struggling to find a foothold in the strange but welcoming city, Murugan was able to rent a small place and settle his family, which now consisted of Selvi, son Kumareshan and daughter Tamilarasi. Life was reasonably good with friendly and helpful neighbours and freedom from the restrictions imposed by the limited opportunities back home. He had no complaints with life. Selvi and he worked hard day and night, setting aside a part of their savings month on month at a local bank, to fulfil their dreams. They had indeed planned their finances well.

Murugan always dreamt of using the small portion in the front of his home to set up Murugan Selvi Snacks, where he would be serving hot idlis, vadas, and filter coffee at affordable prices to the neighbourhood folks. He had also visited Coimbatore a few months back to check on wet grinders of various sizes, mixers, brass utensils, large boilers and coffee filters to adorn his eatery. He wanted to create the same ambience in Dharavi as he was used to seeing as a young boy in the various hotels lining the Madurai – Tirunelvelli highway.

The time to translate his dream to action was finally a few weeks away, when his Recurring Deposit would become payable. Selvi had been excited and was regularly informing her's and Murugan's parents about their eatery and its inauguration just a few weeks away. She was imploring them to visit and bless her, Murugan, and their kids for a bright future.

Murugan Selvi Snacks was to open during Deepavali, the auspicious festival of lights. Every rupee saved by them for every month during the past Three years in their Recurring Deposit was to mature well in time before the grand day of their life. Murugan and Selvi had truly arrived in this city, after a struggle of nearly a decade. There was no stopping them. So, they felt greatly assured…..

03

SHATTERING OF A MOTHER'S DREAM

In a distant suburb of the city, life for a family was becoming a virtual seesaw.

Sneha Dalvi was a happy and bubbly young lady, living in her own world with her daily dose of afternoon soap operas on TV. Her husband was a bus conductor and earned a handsome salary to take care of the needs of the family. Their eldest son, Abhijit, was born within a year of their marriage, and the younger one, Aneeket, was born after a gap of nearly eight years. Theirs was a happy family, not financially well off, but they were able to look after themselves reasonably well, within Dalvi's salary and at the subsidised living quarters provided by his employer.

Then, during the deluge in the city some five years ago, Dalvi developed a fever which refused to go away. All medications proved futile. Finally, after elaborate tests, he was diagnosed with a strange strain of Swine fever. His health started deteriorating and he started gradually losing weight. Once a healthy young man, Dalvi became a shadow of his former self. He was now all skin and bones. Sneha did her best to humour him and nourish him back to health. All her efforts were proving futile and she was losing against the dreaded disease. The family's savings was also fast depleting. Dalvi's employers were understanding and gave his full salary along with medical reimbursements. Later, owing to his long absence, they started giving him half the salary and, finally, had to give him leave without pay.

Sneha had withdrawn dry from her husband's Provident Fund balance to take care of the family's daily needs and his medical bills. At last, after fighting for nearly a year, both Sneha and Dalvi gave up. He passed away peacefully one night. The happy and cheerful family was pushed to the wall with nowhere to go.

Just then, a glimmer of hope appeared in the form of Dalvi's employers giving Sneha a job on compassionate grounds. For the first time in her life, she started travelling long distances for work, leaving her two sons to manage themselves.

Sneha's travel from one end of the city to another and long work hours left her no time to be with her children when they needed her the most. To her surprise and relief, Abhijeet became responsible overnight. He had seen his mother going through hell in the past one year. Once a cheerful and beautiful mom, she had suddenly begun to grow old, with silver hair and dark circles under her eyes. He started waking up early and helping her with the household chores. He took care of himself and his younger sibling.

Years passed by, and the family that struggled to pick up the pieces of their life, finally began to settle down. Abhijit supplemented the household income by taking tuition for lower classes. Sneha was in silent admiration of her boys, who rallied around her during the most trying times in her life. Abhijeet had done well in his XIIth and was soon to get admission into college. Aneeket was also doing well in academics with the full support of his older brother. Each one, in their own way was trying to bounce back.

Sneha knew that Abhijit was sacrificing all the dreams that a youngster of his age had. He was an ideal son and had done everything possible that his young mind could assess of the situation. Now, she wanted his college days to be pleasant. She had seen him riding his friend's bike with a twinkle in his eye. She had often seen him outside the bike showroom in the neighbourhood. However, knowing the financial plight of the family, he had never made this interest known to his mother.

Nothing would give her more happiness than to see Abhijit ride a bike of his own. She was to make it happen, and had applied for a festival advance from her employer. She had placed the funds in a short term fixed deposit with the bank, so that the funds do not get used for any other purpose. The FD would mature a week before Abhijit was to turn eighteen. She wanted to surprise him and cherish the glee in his eyes when she would hand over the keys of the bike to him.

Sneha was waiting for the day, which would erase the struggling memories of the past years from Abhijit's mind forever. She knew that her wait would be over soon. So, she felt greatly relieved with the mere thought……

04

LIFE SAVINGS OF AN NRI WIPED OUT

In yet another corner of the city, one more story of despair and hope was beginning to unfold.

Alfred Raju already seemed like an old man. Though he was in his forties, no one would believe that he was a year younger than fifty five. After graduating in Science from the University of Mumbai in the early eighties, Alfred worked as a badli (contract) worker at a Chemical Company in the distant suburb of Vasai. There were times when he got to work on all days of the month, and then there were hard times, when he was called in to work for just four to five days in a month.

Every day was a struggle and full of anxiety. There was never enough for the family of five, comprising of himself, his aged parents, younger brother and sister. After a lockout was declared at the mill where his father worked, the entire burden of the family fell on Alfred's shoulders. His siblings were still in college. Alfred had to report early at the Chemical Company and during his train journey, he unfailingly went through the Employment Times that he bought once a week. He scrutinised the weekly paper several times for any possible opportunity to get a more stable job that would pay him a fixed monthly income.

Finally, lady luck seemed to shine, and there was a glimmer of hope. There was an advertisement tucked in the last page of the Employment Times inviting applications from Chemistry Graduates to work as plant operators at an oil rig in Dubai's high seas, managed by Dubai Petroleum. The salary was good and tax free, and the perks were excellent too. However, the work was strenuous. The plant operator needed to be cut away from the world and be on call at the rig in the high seas with treacherous weather conditions, for a continuous period of twenty eight days. This was followed by a break of twenty eight days of paid leave along with a free passage to their home country. Alfred was undeterred by the hazard the job posed. He was up for any challenge.

Alfred applied for the post on the very same day and was called for a test and an interview within a few weeks. He cleared the test and interview, and was off to Dubai even before he could come to terms with the rapid changes in his life. Dubai, and a job in the high seas, beckoned him.

Thus began the long innings of nearly a decade, when he was away from the family for twenty eight days in a month followed by visit home for twenty eight days. While at home during the break, to everyone's surprise, he would be so very tired that he would sleep most of the days. Life in the high seas was taking a toll on his body clock.

Alfred started earning a tax free income in petrodollars. Everyone in the family was happy with their new found prosperity. A small flat gave way to a large two Bedroom, Hall and Kitchen flat, replete with a modular kitchen, flat TV, music system, furniture, fixtures, and gadgets that made life comfortable for all.

In the Midst of it all his brother got admission in an expensive hotel management institute, his sister's wedding was celebrated in a grand manner, and Alfred himself was getting ready to marry his childhood girlfriend.

Though everyone in the family was happy with the new found prosperity, Alfred was his shadowy self. His work pressure and constant change in weather was affecting his health beyond repair. While at work in the high seas, he had to slog, and often got just a few hours of sleep before the siren went off due to a technical snag and it was time for him to attend to it. The initial days at the high seas were very difficult and when he was on a twenty eight day break back home, there were several occasions when he felt like sending his resignation to his employer from India. However, when he saw that his income was bringing happiness to the entire family, who had only witnessed struggle all their lives Alfred would brush aside his thoughts of resigning.

Months and years passed by, and the depreciation of Indian Rupee against UAE Dirham meant that his Dirham income could fetch more Rupees than it did earlier. Alfred had got used to his twenty eight day onshore and offshore routine.

Alfred was smart. He knew that life in the high seas could be unpredictable and employment in the oil rich gulf country offered no job security. Every new plant head brought with them new ways to cut costs and, thereby, increase their own increment and bonus. Alfred had to make good while time lasted.

Having seen financial struggle quite early in life, he had started saving in high interest bearing Rupee denominated NRE Fixed Deposits. Every month he opened an NRE FD and, in no time, his savings and interest thereon ballooned to a sizeable savings nest. He never withdrew his FD on its maturity. He went on renewing the same, so that when the time came for him to call it a day to the life in the high seas, he would have enough savings to fall back on. With its interest income alone, he could take care of his aged parents and his own family consisting of wife, Rita, and school going son, Ralph.

On one of his twenty eight day offshore breaks, he was discussing his plans of soon coming back for good. He reassured his parents and family that by GOD's grace he had enough savings and that he would be investing a small portion of the savings in setting up ARR Travel and Tourism Company – his own travel firm. His parents and family were very supportive of his ideas. They knew that when it came to financial planning, Alfred was smart and savvy. So, they sincerely believed……

05

WORTHY SON IS FORCED TO FAIL IN HIS DUTY

Elsewhere in the cosmopolitan part of the city, one more family was making the city its adopted home and shaping its character as the fabled city where dreams come true.

Harshal Dave was the son of a tailor. Harshal came from a humble background. His parents, Himmat Bhogilal Dave and Varshaben, had migrated to the city in late 60s from Morbi village in Kutch. Though not academically educated, Himmatbhai was hard working and always satisfied his customer's demand by stitching the latest trends in dresses.

On arriving in the city, he had rented a small room at a chawl in the suburbs of Mulund. Being street smart, he selected Mulund for its Gujarati neighbourhood. He knew that Varsha would be happy with his choice of location as it also had many households preparing and selling papad, pickles, and Gujarati cuisine. Though the room was small and they had to use a common toilet along with the other residents of the chawl, they considered it a minor inconvenience to bear for experiencing the pleasure of living at a mini Morbi in Mumbai.

Right from 8 am until 10 pm, with short breaks for lunch and tea, Himmatbhai would go on sewing with his hand operated Singer Machine. Festival days of Navaratri and Deepavali were the happiest times for his customers, but for Himmatbhai, it meant working continuously for 18 to 20 hours a day, for weeks at a stretch. He was very jovial and customer friendly. He never knew how to say a 'no' to his patrons, how so ever demanding their specific requirements were.

Years rolled by. Himmat and Varsha became proud parents to Harshal. The child was their bundle of joy. Himmat started working even harder, and Varsha took Harshal to the neighbourhood papad making micro unit. She, with other women from Gujarat, earned a respectable amount each month for rolling papads at a place and time convenient to them.

The daily sessions were full of fun for these women, who forgetting their stress for the few hours that they were together, sang folk songs to bring the flavour of their village to their work place. Harshal and other kids grew up in this homely and secure atmosphere, listening to songs of the makhan chor Krishna and the ideal Rama. Tradition and values were thus effortlessly passed on by the women to their children. These values were to help the children become well-grounded, family oriented teenagers and adults.

Himmatbhai and Varsha wanted to give the best of everything to their Harshal. They wanted him to be educated at the best of schools, wear a smart uniform, and eat healthy food. Their entire life revolved around Harshal and his growing up needs.

Himmatbhai now engaged two more assistants. He also graduated from a hand sewing machine to the foot operated one, which was effortless and easy to use. He and Varsha became prosperous through sheer hard work and frugal living.

Harshal proved to be a worthy son. Always a high performer in school, he also got admission in the best Commerce College in the vicinity. He did not spend much for his studies, preferring to walk to college and come home for lunch. He knew the hardship that his parents underwent to bring him up and yet, never denying him of any requirements for a comfortable life.

Being a clever and hardworking student, Harshal enrolled for Chartered Accountancy and planned to complete both CA and graduation simultaneously. In time, he completed his graduation and CA in the very first attempt. He also got a placement in a leading CA firm close to his residence. Despite being born in a family with limited means, to semi-literate parents, Harshal had come a long way.

Within the first six months at work, Harshal started putting his education to practice. He rented a large flat where his parents could live comfortably. He wanted to improve his parents' standard of living. His father's advancing age and fatigue was visible. Harshal convinced his father to give up the tailoring business, now that he was earning a handsome salary and could afford to give a comfortable lifestyle to his parents.

Harshal had also been regularly saving to take care of any emergency situation and sudden medical expenditure that he may be required to meet. He was especially concerned with his father frequently gasping for breath. He had taken Himmatbhai to the best of cardiologists, only to be told that Himmat was fine, but should not strain himself as he is likely to suffer from a heart attack if he exerted himself.

Harshal had done his homework. He engaged the services of a nurse to help his father with his daily routine. Slowly, Himmat started gaining good health. Harshal and Varshaben were relieved that Himmat had shown signs of good health.

During one of the routine check-ups, the cardiologist suggested to Harshal that while his father was fine, to improve his heart condition, it would be better if a stent was inserted in Himmatbhai's heart. The cardiologist went on to reassure him that the entire procedure would be painless and that Himmat could continue to live a long and healthy life.

The date of the operation was fixed, and everyone was getting mentally prepared. Harshal had also saved enough to provide the best medical treatment that money could buy to his loving father. Varshaben and he did not want to compromise on anything for Himmatbhai, who had been an ideal husband and father.

Varshaben had complete faith that Harshal, her obedient son, would help Himmat to regain his health. Though she was slightly taken aback hearing the expense that Harshal would have to spend, she felt reassured when Harshal said that money was no problem. It was taken care of, and would be available at a short notice from their preferred neighbourhood bank. So, they felt relieved…..

06

GOOD SAMARITAN EMPLOYER HALTS HIS YEARLY GESTURE

In the midst of this all, history was getting rewritten. The city, which had gained notoriety for the communal discord, was setting examples of communal harmony and brotherhood all over again, for which it was well known until the aberration that the carnage brought in the early 90s.

Ishaq Ali had begun life as a peon in a clearing and forwarding company at Sahar. He had the gift of the gab and made friends easily in high places. His bosses were convinced that if at all there was any customer related issue, all they had to do was send Ishaq to resolve it; he would never disappoint them or the customer. Such was the goodwill that he earned with his employers and patrons.

Business at his company was flourishing and Ishaq was a important member of the small team. The company had some of the leading export houses as its customer base. Where other C&F agents struggled to get enough work to stay afloat, Ishaq's company was adding new clients each month and growing its bottom line.

Ishaq's bosses were two Parsi brothers from Cusrow Baug. For them, the C&F business was more of a way to keep themselves active and busy. As they both were growing old and had no one in their family to leave the legacy behind to, they were contemplating an exit from the business to retire to their holiday home in Khandala.

On a long weekend, the brothers called Ishaq to their Khandala holiday home, and broke the news that they were handing over charge of their company to him as a mark of appreciation and acknowledgement of the hard work that he had put in all those years. Ishaq was speechless and overwhelmed. He was deeply touched by this gesture of his bosses, the two brothers, reposing their trust in him and faith in his capabilities. He would never do anything to break their trust.

As per the arrangement, Ishaq was to get 1/3 share of the revenue that he generated from the business and transfer 2/3 to the two brothers.

Ishaq started working even more diligently. He started expanding and employed more staff, whom he handpicked himself. Soon, the company started opening its branches in all other metros and tier 1 cities. Ishaq, being a believer in new technology, started a website and offered online solutions with digital payment options. The customer base grew manifold.

By the end of the decade that Ishaq took over, the company had grown to have Eight branches and nearly 400 staff members. Ishaq was not formally educated. All that he had learnt was on the job and in the field as well as by closely observing his bosses, interacting with his colleagues, team members, customers, bankers, customs officials and competitors in the industry.

He was soon selected as the President of the Western India Clearing and Forwarding Agents Association.

Ishaq was a workaholic and deeply religious. Except for Namaz breaks five times a day, all his time was dedicated to the company and its staff members. He was the first one to report to work and the last one to leave for home to be with his family, comprising of his loving wife, Sultana, and their daughters, Zabin and Raziya.

Ishaq was a firm believer in doing good deeds and was always helpful to his staff members, both in their good and bad times. He regularly gave interest free loans to those facing emergency situations. He also participated in the family functions and celebrations of his staff. When any of his staff members lost their near or dear ones, Ishaq would be with the family to share in their grief.

Ishaq had learnt from his Parsi bosses to treat all his staff members with compassion and understanding. To him, business growth was a natural outcome of the happiness felt by his staff members. Besides giving them practical tips, Ishaq did not interfere with their working. He gave each staff member enough freedom to perform and grow. Thus, he was able to cultivate great team spirit and a sense of belonging in the hearts of each staff member towards the company.

Ishaq believed and respected every faith. Just as he celebrated Id, he also wholeheartedly celebrated Deepavali, Christmas, Pateti, Gurunanak Jayanthi and other religious festivals. Every Deepavali, he wanted his staff to usher in the Goddess of wealth into their families and gave a month's salary to the staff as a special festival bonus. The attrition level at his company was nil, and during exigencies, the staff even volunteered to work extra hours without expecting anything in return.

For Ishaq, the true owners of the company were his staff members and customers. He considered himself a mere enabler and co-ordinator. He took great interest in the well-being of his staff, as they were his extended family.

With Deepavali festival just a month away, as per the usual yearly practice, Ishaq set aside a large part of the earnings in his current account with the bank, so that, just a month before the festival of lights, he could personally handover the special bonus to his staff.

Like in the previous years, Ishaq was waiting to honour a long tradition at his company. It was to give him and his staff great happiness and nothing would steal it away from them. He was absolutely certain that the yearly tradition would continue this year too……

07

ACTRESS PAWNS HER JEWELS TO PAY THE GROCER

Neeta was an accomplished child artist who worked in innumerable Bollywood movies in the early 80s. During her heady days, it was often joked in the Bombay movie industry that she was busier than the leading heroes and heroines. Even after she became a teenager, Neeta made a smooth transition from being a child artist to a sought after leading actress, a feat very few of her contemporary child artists could achieve.

Neeta achieved unparalleled stardom and adulation of her fans. Most of her movies were both critically acclaimed as well as box office hits. She had the Midas touch and could do no wrong. She was thronged by her countless fans, both at the film festivals across the globe, and on the streets of Juhu, Vile Parle, Carter Road as well as in the Mohan, Natraj and Mehboob studios of Mumbai.

Though she acted in many movies as a Doctor, Lawyer or Teacher, in real life, she had to sacrifice her education quite early. This was partly because of her fondness for theatre and silver screen, but mainly due to the avariciousness of her overbearing mother, who did not want to let go of the cash machine that was her daughter.

Inspite of not having a formal education, Neeta was worldly wise and life had taught her a great many lessons. After growing out of her mother's shadow, she married a famous and wealthy director of her times. The marriage was destined to doom, but even by the glamour world's standards, it lasted for a long time – two full years. As a parting gift, Neeta got a sprawling three bedroom apartment at Juhu and more than enough balance in personal account with a bank.

With new faces appearing on the silver screen, Neeta was soon relegated to the role of a side heroine in multi-starrers and gradually to being the elder sister of young heroines, and sometimes, even as a mother to heroes twice her age. Nevertheless, that was the hard reality of the make believe world of cinema, Where heroines generally have a short shelf life.

Neeta started getting fewer and fewer roles, and even those that she got, hardly gave her either the creative satisfaction or the remuneration to justify her status. She was a fighter and not one to give up easily. She was smart enough to know that she had to hold on to her savings and investments in fixed deposits, as those were the only insurance she had to fall back upon, should the roles completely dry up.

The years from the mid 90s leading up to 2010, were years of struggle for the likes of Neeta and many of her colleagues who had seen heydays during the 70s and 80s until the early 90s. Neeta had to think of ways to survive. Her manager advised her that movie making was becoming an unviable commercial venture and nobody would run the risk of engaging the services of the actors of yesteryears. The only option left for actors and actresses of her era was to make a smooth transition into TV serials.

Neeta saw reason in her manager suggestion and started networking with well-known production houses, whose producers had at one time made a beeline to sign her up for their movies.

These producers, now in the business of churning out TV serials by the dozen, could not say no to the one time great Neeta. She started getting roles of a scheming business baroness and an outright cruel mother-in-law in TV serials. It was a far cry from her nice to a fault kind of movie roles. Yet, Neeta was not complaining. The serials kept her busy and the kitchen fire burning. Although her fee was considerably lower, nonetheless, it gave her an opportunity to be in circulation and enjoy the recall value in the collective memory of her fans.

Neeta was enjoying her new found lease of reel life. While the paltry fees from her work in serials took care of her lifestyle, her bank investments gave her a steady monthly income to lead a comfortable life. At times, when she had little or no work, she reflected that for a girl once belonging to the lower middle income group she hadn't done badly in life after all. One sensible step that she took after the separation from her ex-husband was to invest in Fixed Deposits with the bank. The returns were not high, but at least, they were regular and steady.

Little did she realise that all this was to drastically change forever with the bank, the custodian of her wealth, going bust. She would be unable to pay her Manager and soon would be required to borrow money from her friends to survive.

With her high maintenance lifestyle, even her friends stopped lending her money and soon stopped taking her calls. That was the time, Neeta, finding herself alone and not knowing what to do, was compelled to pawn her jewels – her proud possessions – to raise money to survive and pay for her daily needs and extraordinarily high maintenance.

Neeta had faced many ups and downs in her over 40 years of professional life, but for the first time, she was facing financial challenges just like thousands of the bank's other customers customers. She was sure that her bank would soon re-open and her woes would come to an end. However, each day was proving to be a drag.

She started attending sit-downs, dharnas and even giving interviews on popular TV channels, thinking that highlighting her plight to the world would somehow make the authorities take notice and come up with solutions to ensure a happy ending to the financial crunch faced by thousands like her, much like the happy endings in most of her movies. But this was real life. Her conviction was based on years of her association with the tinsel town and make believe world, but for once, the real world had pulled the rug from under her feet and she, like thousands of others, had no clue how to survive….

08

HOUSING SOCIETY'S REDEVELOPMENT PLANS GET STALLED

The cluster of buildings collectively known as Sher-e-hind housing society, had all their operative accounts as well as fixed deposits earmarked for various purposes with their preferred bank. The relationship went back to nearly four decades and had commenced when the bank had just started its operations with a few branches in the city. The promoters of the Society, its first Managing Committee, and every succeeding Managing Committee, continued and enhanced their relationship with the bank over the years.

In a way, the fortune of the residents of the housing society was closely tied with that of the bank. Almost all the residents had their Savings, Fixed Deposits, Recurring Deposits, Lockers and multiple relationships with the bank. The youth of the many homes in the society had also availed two wheeler loans, car loans, home loans and business loans from the bank. The residents also took various insurance policies through the bank, and bought foreign exchange whenever they went on overseas tours. It was more than a mere savings or fixed deposit relationship.

For the two hundred residents of Sher-e-hind, it was their 'ghar ka bank'. As the branch of the bank, with an in-house ATM, was within a walking distance of less than five minutes from their society, the residents never kept more than few thousand rupees at home, always preferring to withdraw from the 24x7 ATM or use the net banking facility of the bank to move funds to and fro.

The society was built in the early 70s with funds pooled by the initial members. Due to the lack of availability of quality cement and steel in the India of the 70s, the quality of construction of the society was, at best, average. The financial capacity of each member did not make it affordable for them to build large flats. Hence, the flats were of 1 bedroom, hall and kitchen with just 1 toilet and bathroom. Each floor had a common balcony which doubled up as a bedroom for households with multiple children.

Life in the society was functional but full of fun, with the spirit of caring and sharing amongst all. Privacy was neither possible nor expected in such a community living atmosphere. Celebrations and festivals were open for all and did not need any special invitation to attend. Exam results, job interviews and appointments, matrimonial arrangements, child birth, anniversaries, phone or cooking gas connections, purchase of a TV or Fridge or even bereavement in anyone's family, saw the participation and involvement of every resident of the society.

Elders of the society took it upon themselves to admonish wayward youngsters and celebrate the academic and professional achievements of the meritorious, as if it was achieved by one of their own. Such was the oneness and inseparable bond amongst the residents of the society. All of them had known each other for over 40 years through their ups and downs.

With the passage of time, the wear and tear of the society, lifestyle changes, requirement for more space as well as affordability and affluence of each member of the society, most of the third generation members felt a need to redevelop their society so that they too could give their children an ambience similar to that offered by the new apartments which had sprung up in the vicinity. Though the first and second generations did not mind living as a community, the next generation felt it was an apologetic lifestyle, which needed a change, in keeping with their affluence.

Talks of re-development had gathered momentum during the past two years. With the availability of the additional Floor Space Index and Transfer of Development Rights, the members of the Society decided to pass a resolution in the Annual General Meeting, to have a swanky new Society in the place of the original one.

The Sher-e-hind Managing Committee members did not want to compromise on the quality of construction or aesthetics of their new society. The members had known each other all their life and also had many qualified engineers, planners, draftsmen, and contractors within their group. The members of the Managing Committee thus decided to pool in-house resources to self-redevelop their society instead of handing over the project to an outside builder. The Society was also flush with the funds parked at their 'ghar-ka-bank'.

The self-redevelopment was going on in full swing. Intimation of Approval and Commencement of Construction certificates were obtained from the office of the Municipal Corporation. Different agencies were shortlisted and negotiations were completed. Legal and project monitoring firms were selected. Performance guarantee was obtained from the various vendors, financial plans were drawn up, and consent of all was recorded. An agreement for alternate accommodation as well as for the new flat was drafted and registered.

Help was provided to each member for the transfer of their personal effects, and and thirty six post-dated rent cheques were given from the Society's a/c to each member, to pay the monthly rent of their alternate accommodation. In the days leading to the vacating of their homes, Members of the society met each other had one grand dinner party on the terrace of the society, and took innumerable group photos and selfies with their best friends. As the last of the members left the Society, electric meters were surrendered, and demolition work commenced.

Within weeks, the cluster of Sher-e-hind society was razed to the ground. Members would frequently visit the location where their society once stood. They had mixed feelings of losing the life-long memories attached to their society, but they brushed such thoughts aside as they would be getting a much bigger and convenient flat with modern amenities within just three years. They consoled each other saying Three years would pass soon, go in a jiffy and that to get something good in life, one needs to put up with minor inconveniences.

The Bhoomi Puja before commencement of the construction was fixed for a Sunday. Members were asked to attend with their families. The physical form of Sher-e-hind society had disappeared, however, the members had vehemently decided to keep the spirit of their togetherness alive. A large cut-out of the proposed building greeted everyone at the site.

An in-house CA firm was assigned the duty of managing the allocation of funds. The funds from the bank account were apportioned towards each work. Everything was well planned and executed to the minutest detail. Just a weekend was left to embark upon the project. Nothing would now take away the resolve of the Society members to give birth to a New Sher-e-hind Housing Society. They would not have believed that within a matter of just 48 hours, their sacrifices and plans would go awry…

09

SENIOR CITIZEN IS MADE TO BEG FOR MEDICINES

Sadrangani was in her 80s, facing old age related ailments but still fiercely independent, both physically and financially. She had been a no nonsense woman all her life. After losing her husband within a few years of her marriage, she vehemently refused proposals brought by her well-meaning relatives for remarriage. Instead, she concentrated on pursuing teaching, which was her ambition, but had taken a backseat due to her marriage. With the passing away of her husband and without any children of her own, she felt that the teaching profession would give her happiness, money, and the love of children, even if they were not her own.

She was a graduate in English Literature and had an immense love for English Grammar, Prose, Poetry, Comprehension, Precis, Essay writing, etc. She finished a teaching course, which qualified her to be a high school teacher. Within no time, she got a well-paying job at a Convent School run by an educational Trust.

Sadrangani gave all her time and energy to teaching the subject the way she was taught by her own high school teachers. Soon, the students started falling in love with the subject and the language. Their new teacher was unlike any other teacher they had known. She had a way with her students, and was more of a friend to them than a stern teacher. To her, language was a bridge that connected people and, hence, the phonetics and nuances of the language had to be well understood. Her aim was to help her students communicate effectively throughout their life time.

The students did not want her lecture to end as she narrated stories and anecdotes of each author, poet and poetess. If one of her lessons was taken from the collection of short stories written by Ernest Hemingway or O Henry, she would go into the events that shaped their life, thought process and writing style. If a poem of Christina Rossetti was melancholic, Sadrangani would give so much information on the poetess who died young, that the students would never forget either the poem or the poetess. Such was the dedication of the teacher and her rapport with her students.

After working for nearly thirty years, Sadrangani retired from her teaching profession at the age of sixty. She carried plenty of lovely memories of her students and colleagues. She also received termination benefits in the form of Provident Fund and Leave Encashment.

Sadrangani invested the funds with the bank as she received an attractive interest rate and also 1% more under the Senior Citizen deposit scheme of the bank. One of her students working at the bank implored her to invest her funds with the bank.

She invited her unmarried younger sister and brother to live with her, just the way they had lived together in their youth. The three of them were getting old and wanted to be of assistance to each other. At her suggestion, both her sister and brother also placed their savings with the bank under a high interest earning fixed deposit.

The interest income from the FD was enough to take care of their monthly expenses and medical needs.

Life for Sadrangani and her siblings was going on smoothly without much of a stress. She passed her time reading books of her favourite authors, while her sister was glued to the daily soaps, and her brother was in his own world with the daily newspaper and old Bollywood songs from the golden 60s playing in the background.

Their limited wants, uncomplicated living style, and ability to pay for their needs and medicines made them lead a life of dignity and self-respect. They had no inkling that very soon they would be required to compromise on their principles and seek help from their relatives and friends, even for their daily medicines and other essentials. Even in their wildest dreams, they would not have imagined that a day would come, when, despite having enough savings in their bank account, they would still have to reluctantly ask for help to lead their lives and buy basic necessities.

Though they had faced many hardships and challenges in their lives, they would find themselves to be ill-prepared to handle this sudden upheaval in their lives, for which they would have no answers. Their health neither permitted them to participate in the morchas nor visit their bank to meet the administrator or drop in to the regulator's office to present their case. Every day was becoming a living hell for Sadrangani and her siblings . In the evening of their lives, all they wanted was to have a peaceful existence, which fate was to deny to them.

HOSPITAL TRUST'S FUNDS GET BLOCKED

A twenty bed Eye hospital had been running efficiently for the past four decades. The hospital was funded by common people with a charitable disposition from the town of Bhuj. Prominent professionals from the community had been giving their time, energy and expertise to the hospital over the years. The noble objective with which it was set up and the nominal amount it charged for its various services, including cataract, retina and glaucoma operations, attracted patients from all strata of the society. Thanks to the regular stream of charity, the hospital could boast of latest equipment, and services of the best in class surgeons and ophthalmologists. All the departments were ISO certified and the end to end process, from registering a patient until the complete check-up and discharge, was smooth and pleasant.

The hospital had accumulated enough funds in its bank account and had drawn up plans to increase the bed capacity by purchasing additional space in the vicinity of the hospital. All plans were in place to expand operations. Interviews were conducted to get additional administrative and support staff on board. Advance payment was made to acquire the property to put up additional beds. Final payments were planned after the Shradh period, Which the traditional trustees considered to be an inauspicious time to begin any new venture.

Everyone was excited. Brochures and leaflets were printed, announcing the opening of an eye hospital with the latest equipment, high service standards, qualified and experienced doctors and para medic staff, including plans to start a hospital-on-wheels to cater to patients in far off villages. Truly, a hospital which started as a single bed unit forty years ago, had now grown to serve patients far and wide at an affordable tariff. It was only a matter of days before it would become well known.

Despite the noble work being carried out by the hospital and its ambitious future plans, it became the talk of the town within days before the launch of its annexe hospital, but for all the wrong reasons. News had spread thick and fast that the hospital was struggling to stay afloat. All its deposits had got blocked at the failed bank…

11

SELF-HELP GROUP (SHG) LOSES DEPOSITS OF 'BELOW POVERTY LINE' MEMBERS

The tiny frame of Shakuntala bai would belie anyone into believing that she must be in her late 30s. Though she did not remember her birthday, she did remember that she was married off by her parents on the very next day after the then Prime Minister of the country was gunned down by her bodyguards. Her parents had informed her that she had turned eighteen that year and was fit to get married as per the Warkari custom of her village. The boy selected by her parents was in his mid 20s, pious, stout and strong. He was working in a big city. That is all that she knew of her husband.

After the marriage, she left with her husband to settle in a one room tenement at Parel, the textile hub of Bombay. Dhondu, as he was fondly nicknamed by his friends, was a Mathadi worker (Head Loader). He was hard working, spiritual, a loving husband and, most importantly, had no vices. At a very young age, his parents had initiated him into the Warkari tradition and had placed a black Tilak on his forehead with a string of black beads on his neck. This was to protect him and keep reminding him of the tenets of the Warkari tradition every living moment.

His wife was happy with whatever little income Dhondu earned. Despite limited means, he never forgot to send a Money Order every month to his parents living in the village. He also set aside a small sum of money each month to undertake the yearly customary visit to see his Vithoba at Pandarpur. That year, being the year of his marriage, he took his bride Shakuntala, with pride on a Padhyatra to Pandarpur.

Life for Dhondu and Shakuntala, as also the hundreds of Mathadi workers like them, was generally hard and hand to mouth, but they were never short of happiness, deriving joy from small, daily pleasures. Their life revolved around their family, small circle of friends, daily dawn to dusk work and Abhangs in praise of their Vithal and Rakhumai. They would do kirtans in the local train on their way to work and, on Sundays, at the home of one of the members of the community.

Within five years of their marriage, they were blessed with two children. Ganpat was the eldest and Shaila, his kid sister. The family of Dhondu and Shakuntala was complete and content. However, both of them also realised that their meagre income would not suffice the needs of their growing family and meet the additional monthly expenses.

Shakuntala, after her initial inhibitions with the big city, was soon getting used to life in the cosmopolitan city. With an affable nature and genuine networking skills, making new friends came naturally to her. She discussed with Dhondu that she could contribute to the family's income by taking up household work in the area. She had also requested a senior couple in her neighbourhood, hailing from her village, to babysit her children for a nominal monthly sum. Dhondu was both thankful and amazed with his wife's eagerness and smartness to shoulder the financial burden of their family.

For a village bred Shakuntala, household work was not stressful at all. She excelled in cleaning the vessels, washing and drying clothes, and sweeping the floor. Her employers liked her honesty, punctuality, and also, unlike others, she neither gossiped nor availed frequent leaves, except for her annual visit to Pandarpur.

She got into her employer's good books with her simplicity, truthfulness and integrity. She was soon referred by her employers to their friends and had enough work at multiple households from morning till late evening. The income of both Dhondu and Shakuntala, took care of all their immediate needs and duties towards their aged parents in their native village.

However, they knew that with the growth of their children, their demands and expenses would also grow and, hence, there would be a need to save each month for the children's education and marriage as well as their own old age.

Their neighbourhood, comprising of by-lanes of Lalbaug, Ganesh Gulli, Curry Road, Chinchpokli and Elphinstone, were made up of thousands of hard working people like them, who collectively formed the underbelly of the great metropolis and financial capital of the country. This large segment of the society helped the more privileged citizens by carrying out their day to day menial and labour intensive workload. Whether offering the services of a housemaid or preparing food, cleaning the house, babysitting children, washing the family cars, walking their pets or ensuring that the lunch boxes of their customers were picked up from the homes to be delivered to the various offices in time and without any error, all these tasks were efficiently handled by an army of labourers like Dhondu and Shakuntala, and the world renowned Bombay Dabbawallas, who collectively comprised of the bottom of the society's food chain.

Though during the early years of their entry into the city, they had to fend for themselves and take whatever their employers would pay them, during the course of the last two decades, the workers' union had sprung up across various pockets of the city. By paying a small membership fee and investing in the share capital of the credit society, a labour could enlist in a union and the credit society, which were part of a large apex body with presence across various industries. The union helped its members by formulating basic human rights policies and by regulating wages for various types of work, fixing hours of work, mandatory leaves, minimum wage, bonus, dispute resolution, etc.

The credit society provided financial literacy to its members and accepted small monthly deposits, which were invested with banks.

Loans were offered to members within short notice at no security and at an interest rate that was better than the 3% per month levied by the many Afghan Pathans roaming the streets of the neighbourhood. Members of the Credit Society, who needed financial assistance to meet their urgent physical exigencies, marriages in the family, hospitalisation, education, purchase of white goods, etc., would avail of such loans at regular intervals.

The responsibility of overseeing and managing the financial wing of the union was entrusted to a committee of hand -picked senior members of the union, supported by the advice of a Chartered Accountant who also hailed from the community. The responsibility of investing the vast pool of funds, making available loans, collecting the interest and principle, conducting monthly meetings and yearly annual general meetings, as well as declaring dividends on the share capital to the members, were all efficiently handled by the office bearers.

Although the investment in shares and deposits by each member was relatively low, the regular contribution by hundreds of thousands of the labour force helped the corpus fund to assume gigantic proportions. Each month, the

Credit Society would invariably collect over a Crore of rupees through such small deposits from its members.

The lot of the members had considerably improved after the formation of the Credit Society. The Society had also set aside a mini-fund to provide loans at very nominal rates to meet medical expenses incurred towards curing terminal diseases of members and also for meeting funeral expenses, in case of death in the family of a member. The thousands of labourers, who had toiled day and night, were secure in their belief that their relocation to the city from their villages many years back was the best decision of their lives. Though life in the city was tough, their living standards had improved through the years, and they were sure that their Credit Society would take care of their retirement by returning their deposits with interest along with their contribution to the Share Capital and accrued dividend on the same.

The Managing Committee of the Credit Society was highly respected and enjoyed the goodwill of each member. Their financial acumen and attention to detail was well appreciated by the members. For them, those who managed the Credit Society were GOD's chosen workers, the enlightened lot, and therefore could do no wrong.

Their perception was to change soon. The vast corpus fund of hundreds of the poorest of the poor like Dhondu and Shakuntala, saved over decades, was to get stuck forever. The failed bank was to earn the curse and wrath of thousands of hard working, simple migrant labourers. For them, the act of the bank and its large loan sharks stealing their hard earned money, saved little by little with their Credit Society, over the years like a sparrow, was similar to someone stealing the coins placed at the mouth of the corpse. In their eyes, this type of a financial misappropriation was the lowest form of treachery and crime. Overnight, the life of Dhondu and Shakuntala and thousands like them, became topsy turvy….

12

COMMUNITY GETS A RUDE SHOCK EXCOMMUNICATES TOP OFFICIALS

The community is known the world over for its valour, hard work, helpful nature, large heartedness, zest for life, discipline, unwritten law of never to beg for alms, and abstinence from vices as well as for paying respects to the elders, religious heads and scriptures.

This year was going to be special as it was the 550th birth anniversary of the Great Guru, the teachings of whom are revered by people across the country and around the world.

Plans were drawn up to conduct many social events to coincide with the anniversary. Health camps, cataract eye operations, wheel chair donations to the needy, Langar to feed thousands of devotees from the common community kitchen, sponsoring of higher education of the girl child, donations of, reading lamps, laptops, setting up of old age homes and even a veterinarian nursing home on wheels to attend to street strays, were all meticulously planned.

Teams were formed, areas earmarked, and responsibilities delegated to each member of the respective teams. Security arrangements, closed circuit cameras, drinking water arrangements, first aid kits, ambulance vans, footwear stands, a separate seating arrangement for the senior citizens, valet parking and loudspeakers were getting installed at strategic locations. Uniformed boys and girls getting trained in soft skills and crowd management techniques were all being put in place.

Long-term Deposits and Investments were getting converted to short term deposits. Dates to withdraw them just in time, closer to the week of the event, was diarised with clockwork precision by the Managing Trustees and the instructions were percolated to the team of Treasurers, handling each aspect of the event.

The sheer size, grandeur and logistics involved in anticipating challenges and coming up with multiple solutions well in advance to resolve every possible scenario, would need great analytical skills and visionary acumen. Hundreds of team members were working ten to twelve hours every day, for months on end, at the many community centres across the city. They were highly organised, energetic and had a common purpose – that of ensuring the big event gets celebrated in a manner that befits such a once-in-a-century occasion, commemorating the birth of their revered Guru.

Each team member had set aside their other commitments and pursuits, to give their complete attention to celebrating their Guru's birth anniversary.

The big event saw many of their overseas members planning a visit to the country to participate in the grand event. It was to be a week-long celebration across the country. Committee members from each city were exchanging notes to ensure that the event is celebrated in a uniform manner, without any jarring note. The sub-committees in the financial capital of the country had an additional responsibility of making good any financial shortfall faced by the committees from the other cities. The treasury teams of the city were well prepared to handle any exigencies from their colleagues in the other parts of the country. Though they were geographically apart, all of them were committed to the single cause of making sure that their Guru's birthday celebration was an occasion to remember and cherish for a very long time.

The grand event was just a month away, when the Chief of the city's committee received a frantic call from one of his treasurers. He was blabbering and incomprehensible. He was heard sobbing at the other end of the line. Suddenly, the landline started ringing. One more member of the inner committee broke the news that the bank having the entire funds of the Committee has been slapped with restrictions by the Reserve Bank of India. He went on to say that no one would be allowed to withdraw their money from that very moment. Crowds had gathered in front of the bank's branches and every channel was reporting a big scam at the bank. The CEO had called for a press meet to explain the reasons for the restrictions imposed by the regulator. He was comforting the depositors that everything would be fine and that the bank was strong enough to come out of the situation in just about 6 months.

The next day saw mayhem at the Committee's office. No one knew how to react to a situation that they had not even remotely factored or dreamt in their wildest dreams. Every activity was waiting for attention and release of funds. It was an emergency situation and needed quick thinking on the part of everyone in the organising committee.

The head of the Commemorative Committee abruptly got up and left for the HO of the bank to meet the administrator appointed by the regulator. He was ushered in without any waiting time. On meeting the administrator, he brushed aside the pleasantries and pointedly asked the administrator how long would it take to get access to the funds of the Committee, realistically. When he was told that it could take a few months to a year or even more to assess the scale of the fraud, arrive at a fair value of the assets and finally get buyers to buy those assets before eventually returning the depositors money, the Committee's head knew instantly that the Birth Centenary event for their Guru had hit a terrible road block.

Without waiting to hear more, he left as abruptly as he had entered, to meet other committee members and apprise them of what he had learnt from the administrator. On his way out, he saw the group photographs of the beaming Chairman and the Board of Directors prominently displayed on the wall. He quickly clicked a photo of the same with his smart phone.

On reaching his office, he asked his secretary to convene an urgent meeting with the members of his core team, the heads of various sub-committees, the Treasurer, the Board Secretary and prominent seniors of the community.

At the quickly convened meeting, the head of the Commemorative Committee broke the news that nearly 75% of all their liquid funds that were placed with their primary bank had got stuck due to the bank's failure. The moratorium on it by the regulator would make it impossible to withdraw the same before the birth anniversary.

The committee considered the funds available with the other banks, vis-a-vis the approximate fund requirements for each of the planned activities. Priorities were reworked along with list of donors who could be approached for funding. However, most of such donors were also banking with the failed bank and, hence, any chance of receiving donations from them were felt to be bleak. Left with no other solution in sight, the committee reluctantly passed a resolution deciding to tone down the celebrations and keep the events and expenses to the bare minimum.

The committee also unanimously passed one more resolution, that of condemning the fraudulent behaviour of the Chairman and the Board of Directors of the failed bank. The resolution strongly condemned the Chairman and many of the Board Members, who were themselves prominent heads of the community, for letting such a calamity befall on the customers of the bank and the common people.

Without a shred of doubt or reluctance, the resolution excommunicated the Chairman and Board Members from their community, and also stripped them from the various honorary posts they held in the various sub-committees. The resolution went on to restrict their entry and participation in any of the events during the birth centenary celebrations of their Guru. Though legal proceedings would take a few years to pronounce them guilty, the Commemorative Committee had taken a decision to hand out the harshest possible punishment to the Chairman and the Board for letting down their customers and for failing to uphold the tradition of the community's unblemished service to the Society. It was possibly the most definitive step, taken swiftly to name and shame the perpetuators of the heinous crime. Nothing would ever redeem them from such a mighty fall from grace.

13

IN A TRIPLE WHAMMY, SENIOR CITIZEN LOSES EVERYTHING

One has to be unlucky to face a financial situation that results due to the failure of a bank. On top of it, if the person is required to pay tax claims, he should be terribly unlucky to face this double whammy. But what would one say to Septuagenarian Bharucha, who with one stroke of hard luck, not only lost his life savings, but along with it also lost access to the sale proceeds of his property as well as the funds parked in the bank to pay the capital gains tax on the sale? Not only that, to top it, the retirement home where we was looking forward to spending the rest of his life, also lost all its funds that were kept with the bank to pay for the day to day operations of the home.

Bharucha was a banker himself and had worked hard for over thirty five years at one of the public sector banks. He had taken good care of his aged parents, sacrificing his own personal life and priorities. Nevertheless, he was a very happy and content man, having performed his duties towards his parents, employer and customers, diligently.

In the year 2010, after losing both his parents in quick succession, Bharucha had nothing much to look forward to. His job at the bank kept him going. He had earned a well-deserved retirement three years back, after serving his bank for nearly thirty five years.

It was as if he had found new freedom. He felt like a great burden was taken off his shoulders. There was no more checking of ledgers or tallying of cash. Finally, he could afford to wake up late, walk up to the Irani café at the extreme end of the Dadar Parsi Colony, have maska pav and tea at a leisurely pace, gossip with Mehernosh at the cash counter and tread back to his home, carrying eggs and a loaf of fresh bread rolled in his favourite Jam-e-Jamshed newspaper of the day.

This was Bharucha's daily routine after retirement. However, his peace was disturbed when Dilip, the local real estate broker, bumped into him at the café one morning. He mentioned in the passing that if ever Bharucha was interested in selling his flat, he could expect a very good price for the same. Also, Dilip mentioned that he could get Bharucha an independent well-furnished room at a retirement home, away from the noise and commotion of the city. The retirement home, run by a Parsi family, would take care of all his needs for a reasonable deposit and a nominal monthly maintenance charge.

Bharucha got hooked on to the idea. After visiting the retirement home along with Dilip, he profusely thanked Dilip for suggesting this wonderful twin solution. He immediately sold his flat to the first buyer, booked a well-ventilated and airy room adjacent to the community kitchen at the retirement home and moved there with his limited possessions. Everything seemed to fall in place.

Life seemed like a dream. His days were spent in peace amongst the flora and fauna at the retirement home. He patted his back for taking the most appropriate decision and included Dilip in his daily prayers. The nominal maintenance charge was settled from the interest income that his FDs with the bank earned him. He had enough money and more, without a care in the world. Life for him was unbelievably perfect.

His CA had advised him to park the sale proceeds of his property at a nearby branch of a bank, which was close to his retirement home, as it was offering a high interest for a short term deposit. He was given an option to either pay the capital gains tax or invest a portion of the sale proceeds in tax saving bonds for five years at nominal returns.

Bharucha, being an upright and duty conscious person all his life, preferred to pay the capital gains tax when it fell due. Until then, he placed the entire sale proceeds along with the tax component of the sale proceeds, with the bank. He reasoned that his tax would go to serve the country in an appropriate manner. In any case, he was left with enough for his daily needs. The retirement home too had their Current Account and Fixed Deposits with the same bank. Hence, it was easy for Bharucha to set up a standing instruction to pay the monthly maintenance fees promptly, on the first of each month.

Every part of the puzzle was getting solved on its own. Then came the Tsunami in the life of Bharucha as well as in the lives of many like him at the retirement home, and in the life of the husband and wife duo managing the home, all of whom had placed their life savings with the nearby bank.

With the bank shutting its doors to the customers and restricting withdrawals from their accounts, all of them suddenly found themselves strapped for cash. With no liquid cash available on their person, even purchasing their day to day groceries became a struggle. They had all their life savings with the bank, but had to still scratch and search for loose change or small notes to pay for the most meagre needs.

Bharucha was the worst hit. He had lost all his savings locked up at the failed bank. On top of that, his capital gains tax payment obligation was coming up soon. He had no idea how he would be able to keep up with the tax obligations, an act he was proud of all his life, that of paying full tax on his income without ever doing tax planning to claim tax rebates or refunds.

The more he thought about his misery, the more sleepless he would get. He was becoming frail with worries. The cheerful nature he possessed during his life, until a few days back, seemed to have vanished. He would keep staring at the ceiling listlessly, not knowing what to make of the turn of events. Praying to the soul of his departed parents and his fire temple, he wished for some solution to emerge.

The caretakers of the retirement home were the gentlest of hosts. Yet, they were forced to inform all their guests that they had barely enough money to run the retirement home for the next 6 months and during this period, if all of them did not experience a divine intervention, they may be required to part ways until the bank permitted them to withdraw their savings.

At their age and with their health conditions, most of the residents of the retirement home were not even able to participate in the various dharnas that were called through WhatsApp groups by all those who had lost their money at the failed bank.

Bharucha and the others at the retirement home had no option but to wait and pray for the light to shine in their lives once again.

14

STUDENTS THE WORST HIT

While the student segment was seemingly the least connected with the failure of the bank, they were, ironically, the most affected by it.

This was largely due to the bank's over drive in packaging and marketing high value education loans. The bank boasted of several tie-ups with Overseas Education Consultancy firms, Full Fledged/Restricted Money Changers and Foreign Exchange Service Providers as well as arrangements with the new generation Private Banks to piggy back on them to market their Global Currency Card and SWIFT platform. The bank went on to enjoy the visibility and loyalty of the student segment, who aspired to get higher education from some of the most prestigious Universities and Business Schools abroad.

The Bank would process education loans in a fasttrack manner, but would levy a exorbitant interest rate on such loans, charge a hefty processing fee, give the most uncompetitive exchange rate and debit the account of the students in an excess of thousand rupees for every SWIFT transmission message.

The students, generally in a tearing hurry to pay the fees to the University and Business Schools, were left with little time to consider other options and would end up coughing high transaction fees on such loans. The students and their parents were willing to put up with all the demands made by the bank, only because the bank would keep up its commitment and the staff would offer excellent customer service.

The day the bank's CEO addressed the press and accepted that the bank had been slapped with moratorium, and that normal banking services would no longer be available, all hell broke loose at the many homes of the students who had either left for their education as per the schedule of the Fall Intake at some of the Universities, or who were on the verge of flying in Oct/Nov to attend their classes in the forthcoming Spring schedule.

Frantic calls were made all over the place to Admin Departments of the overseas Institutions and to close family and friends. No one could quite come to terms with what had befallen them or how to handle this sudden bouncer out of the blue.

On the morning of Monday, the first working day after the announcement of the moratorium, many parents had reached the Head Office of the besieged bank quite early to meet the Administrator appointed by the regulator. After a long wait and much requesting and pushing, some of the parents were finally able to meet the Administrator face to face. They were given just 10 minutes to explain their hardship. The Administrator heard the parents with due respect, but remained noncommittal till the end. They could neither read his face nor get any assurance on when the bank would offer its services and release the loans that were already sanctioned but remained to be disbursed. The Administrator was further handicapped as he was not in the mould of a commercial banker. For every request, he would procrastinate and finally offer a typically bureaucratic reply which would mean nothing much.

Despite the parents crying hoarse, the Administrator remained quiet and unmoved. It was difficult to infer his mind or his body language. For the customers, he was indeed proving to be a tough nut to crack. However, in all fairness to him, it could be looked as his occupational hazard. In just few hours of reporting to the HO of the just collapsed bank, he was burdened with so much grief and overwhelming situations faced by the customers, that anyone else in his place would have had an emotional breakdown. However, the man remained stoic all through the day, for the weeks and months to come. He was merely performing the duty of a lame duck Administrator and was doing a pretty good job of it.

The parents finally grouped together and decided to write to the Finance Minister about their woes. Someone from the group suggested a memorandum be given to the Ombudsman, while another felt it would be appropriate to knock on the doors of the Governor. Yet another parent was of the opinion to involve a political heavy weight, who also had experience in the affairs of such banks.

When the final list was drawn after two days, it made a very touching case study. It included cases wherein a student had gotten admission into an IVY league University, but was about to lose the seat if the admission fees did not get paid in less than a month. Then there were cases of a merit holder who had to complete the last semester at the London School of Economics. His parents were distraught. They dreamt of the best for their son and had mortgaged their property to the bank to raise the loan, and were now waiting for the last instalment of the fees to be paid. With the bank shutting its doors on them and with no security to mortgage to other banks, they had no idea how they would manage to remit the fees for their son's last semester.

Then, there was a case of a parent who was transferring monthly funds for the maintenance of his daughter's study in New York. He was speechless. How was he to manage sending the maintenance to his daughter with all his life savings stuck in the Bank. There was a case of parents whose son could not get his International Forex card topped up in time through the failed bank. He had to face the ignominy of borrowing from his classmates until his parents could come up with an alternate arrangement. Yet another parent wondered as to how he would be able to pay for the return fare of his daughter, who was set to come home in less than a month.

If these were not enough, there was a case of a family that had sold its property and deposited the sale proceeds in their account with the bank. It was meant to fund their merit holder daughter's one year study with a prestigious Business School in France. They were frustrated with the thought that their daughter would be compelled to abandon her plans.

These were stray cases at a few branches of the failed bank. Many of the students were yet to realise the full impact of the event that had occurred over the last weekend. With a huge portfolio of educational loans at the bank, there were many such cases waiting to emerge. Most of the affected students were top academic performers and had a brilliant career ahead of them. However, with the bank's Board committing a breach of trust, it seemed to have played a cruel joke on the lives of so many young and promising boys and girls. The loss was not theirs alone or that of their families, but of the nation that got cheated, missing an opportunity to put to use what could have been their exceptional services.

15

EMPLOYEES FIND THEMSELVES IN A CATCH 22 SITUATION

Though the bank had collapsed and dragged with it the future of all its customers and their family members, the condition and fate of the regular employees of the bank had turned pitiable for no fault of theirs.

Except for the Chairman, the Board, the CEO and a few Heads of Department at the HO, most of the other staff members of the Bank, totalling… nearly 99% of its large workforce, were sincere, hard working, dedicated and honest employees. They had given their blood and sweat to the bank. For most of them, it was their first job. As their job at the bank was very satisfying, they had never felt it necessary to look for an alternative. Most of the employees were like proverbial frogs in the well, who feel secure inside the well. Over time, they lose interest in even knowing what the outside world looks like.

The service standards of the staff and officers were recognised as amongst the best in the industry. It was the only bank that boasted of 365 days of service. The look and feel of the bank as well as its ambience, décor, frontage, aesthetics, furniture, customer lobby, latest flat monitors, smart uniforms for all the employees and the works, would give any peer bank a complex.

Yet, today when the bank had collapsed, buried under heavy non-performing assets and covered with dirt and slime, the swanky offices and the paraphernalia seemed farce and hollow. The customers of the bank surely felt nice and enjoyed the ambience, but not at the cost of losing their life savings. They were not prepared for such a trade-off.

Despite the earth shattering event creating a financial mess in their lives, most of the customers still managed to greet and nod in a pleasant manner, when they met the staff and officers of the bank. It was an acknowledgement and testimony of the highest service standards set by the employees that endeared the customers to them. The customers had realised that the work force of the bank was sincere and honest. They were employees for whom the bank was nothing short of being a sanctum sanctorum. However, unfortunately, they were themselves also caught unawares, like the customers, in choppy waters inside a sinking ship.

It was the unbridled greed of the Chairman and the Board, with the active connivance of the CEO and few high ranking officials of the bank, that had brought about its collapse. The employees were not directly responsible for the mess, except that they could have been more vigilant instead of being oblivious to the red alerts and signals, resulting in the ultimate fall of the bank.

Even at the worst of times, the staff of the bank and those of similar banks in the sector, would demonstrate exemplary service standards, putting their counterparts in other PSU, Private and MNC banks to shame. It was for this very reason and the Personal Banking Services rendered in the true sense of the term, that the customers took a liking to such shadow banks, despite so many seemingly better options available to them.

It was a pity that the Chairman and the Board did not fully realise the goodwill and brand loyalty that was being generated in the minds of the customers by the Human Capital of the bank, working tirelessly at the front office and across all departments.

A Board with an earnest approach to banking and a long term vision could have optimally leveraged the full potential of the vast majority of its highly capable team members, to achieve extensive growth in business. However, it was unfortunate that the Chairman and the Board had a rather narrow and limited vision of defrauding the bank and not unlocking the true potential of their bank's team. Despite getting relatively less remuneration in comparison to their counterparts in other sectors, the hours of work and the quality of service rendered by the vast majority of the Co-op bank staff was far superior in comparison with those of other banks.

While it was not uncommon to notice customers being taken for granted and shouted at in some of the PSU banks, in comparison, the customers of the Co-op bank felt pampered, as they were served with a pleasant smile and warmth every time they interacted with the bank's staff.

The Branch Managers of such Co-op Banks knew their customers personally and also participated in the highs and lows of their customer's personal life. The relationship was truly that of a family. At times, when a long queue would get formed during the beginning of the month for cash withdrawals or deposits, the Officers and the Branch Managers would come to help, ensuring that there is no inconvenience or delay in rendering services.

It was such small yet meaningful gestures that went on to create a brand loyalty for the customers of such Co-operative Banks, which no other banks from non-Co-operative sector could easily poach. Today, however, for no direct fault of theirs, most of the employees would face hours of enquiry by the various fact finding agencies.

Even though the bank had ceased all operation, yet the staff and officers had to visit the branch regularly as usual, only to meet their customers and clarify their unending queries in a pleasant manner to the best of their abilities. The Staff were to be paid their salaries as per the approval of the regulator, yet, the salaries getting credited to their savings account had withdrawal restrictions. Thus, the financial condition of the staff members was no different from their customers. While the customers could participate in the many dharnas, the staff could not be part of such protests. They were truly caught between the cracks and found themselves in an unenviable position.

Despite societal pressures that come with the tag of being an employee of a rogue bank, most of the employees had to report for work. Theirs was indeed an ironical situation. With nothing to look forward to each day, they were still required to put on a fake smile and a calm exterior. With the additional financial burden stemming from no salary, the bulk of the employees were finding themselves in a no-win situation.

Most of the employees were in their mid 40s and 50s, with teenage children, home loan instalments and other such regular financial commitments. Though they had a small saving nest, the moratorium made it inaccessible. While the employees were good at their work, the unseen stigma attached to their resume would make them ineligible for jobs at other banks. Most of them had not acquired any special skills to be considered in an alternate industry. They felt shunned and had nowhere to go.

There was irony galore, impacting several segments right from the customers, to the employees, and the entire sector in general . The irony in the lives of the employees could not have been more pronounced as they were required to pay the EMIs on their loans, though there was an embargo on their savings and investments parked with the bank. The customers having Fixed Deposits as well as the employees were required to ironically pay Tax at source, although their deposits and interests thereon were under freeze. It was turning out to be a cruel joke that fate had played on them.

Then, there occurred the mother of all ironies. News started filtering that even as the depositors and employees were facing a daily struggle to survive, the fraudsters who were responsible for bringing so much misery and grief in the lives of millions, were themselves taking a mini vacation and going off to hill stations outside the city. It was alleged that even during the COVID 19 pandemic, when there was a travel embargo on the general population, the scamsters and their family members were being issued 'hard to get' e-travel passes to freely move from one district to the other.

That was not all. There were many more ironies in store. The regulator's staff themselves had indirectly invested their savings through the Employees' Co-op Credit Society in the bank that had collapsed like a pack of cards. It was a case of the King being caught with his pants down.

The high value securities which were literally going for a song, failed to attract any buyers in the depressed market conditions. This added to the woes and further dampened the spirit of the depositors, who were pinning all hopes of getting back their deposits by sale of the collaterals.

With full blown Covid 19 bringing the city to its knees, strict social distancing norms got enforced, restricting the gathering of crowds, whether it was a social event like a marriage celebration or taking part in a funeral. The same extended to the depositors' right to gather and protest peacefully in various parts of the city. The Covid situation, necessitating health advisory, was proving to be the final straw that broke the camel's back.

Each day, the employees had to drag themselves to work, not only to escape the bleak atmosphere at home, but also to be of some help and source of courage and comfort to the many customers who would still visit their branch religiously each day, expecting a miracle to occur and receive their savings locked in the failed bank.

Each day, everyone was waiting for some positive news from the Administrator, the regulator or the market, which frequently came up with the news of an amalgamation or merger of the bank with a stronger bank. Yet, there was nothing concrete taking shape.

In the midst of all these ironies getting played out, it was also now becoming clearer that the ex-official of the regulator hired by the bank as a consultant to 'manage' adhoc assignments, was responsible for mobilising nearly hundred crores of rupees from the regulator's employees' Credit Co-op Society. There was a talk that this official, who knew his way around, had convinced the employees' body at the regulator's office to invest a large chunk with the bank at a premium interest rate.

The employees of both the bank and the regulator were thus affected in their own way due to the machinations of the top brass at the failed bank. This news though, had a silver lining to it. Many employees of the bank would secretly believe that there was still hope as the regulator would pull a rabbit out of the hat, to save the employees' credit society. However, as everyone would come to experience, nothing of this sort would occur.

At the training centres at other banks and at several television debates, the reasons for the failure of the bank and its overall macro and micro impact would get discussed *ad nauseam*. While the plight of the customers would get maximum air time, the same for the vast majority of the employees' would rarely get a mention. It seemed they were being reckoned as collateral damage that occurs whenever such earthquakes erupt in the financial world.

The moral of the story, as far as the employees were concerned, seemed to suggest that it was not merely enough to be good at your work. It was equally important to be vigilant and look for the Telltale marks and signs that would be the first indications that everything may not be right or as healthy as it may seem.

At the end of the session, before breaking for lunch, the Head of the Bench got up to make a brief statement and remind every employee that they should know that Goodwill, Loyalty, Credibility and Trust are the main foundations of Banks, and these are built over a period of many years. However, it takes just a few wrong steps to lose it, never to gain the lost ground again. That's not all. If one institution gets tainted, the effect of the same is sure to rub off on other institutions in the sector, for no fault of theirs. Hence, it is the inherent duty and responsibility of everyone in the Bank to safeguard the reputation of their Bank and that of the entire fraternity across the sector. The employees need to be ever vigilant and alert to ward off any such Bank failures in the future.

16

NO TAKERS FOR THE TAINTED ASSETS

While the books of the bank seemed to suggest that there was enough security and more to back the loan book, one just had to scratch the surface to realise the hopelessness of the situation. It was noticed that there were compromises made in most of the high value loans.

Valuations of the collaterals were unrealistically high, as a result of which the loan to value ratio had got heavily skewed to the detriment of the bank's interests. Adhoc enhancements were given at a drop of a hat, whenever requested for by the borrowers. Over 70% of all the loans could be traced to a single party and thereby, hitting and surpassing all the regulatory ceilings and risk norms recommended for loans to a single party.

Thus, the bank was truly exposing itself to either swim or sink with the fortunes of the single party.

Book debts were over hundred twenty days in contravention of the best practice to restrict the age of debts to less than ninety days to qualify for funding. Similarly, stock statements were rigged indiscriminately. Hence, the drawing power calculation went for a toss. On top of these, temporary overdrafts were given on some pretext or the other. Some of the Directors also moon-lighted as consultants at the offices of large borrowers, thereby engaging in classic two timing and blatant conflict of interest.

Though attempts were made to monetise the assets, the high reserve price combined with the depressed market conditions resulted in no takers for such assets. The bank repeatedly had to bring down the reserve price in an effort to cut costs by taking maximum permissible haircuts. This strategy would eventually backfire, as the buyer and their syndicate would try to hold the bank in a tight bear grip to drive down the price even more, to an unrealistically low level. Everyone in the market seemed to know the bank's desperation in offloading the tainted assets.

A combination of factors resulted in failed attempts at the many physical auctions. With the Covid 19 Pandemic situation restricting free movements, e-auction was being resorted to. Yet, interest from the potential buyers remained subdued.

The bank seemed to have thrown all caution to the wind by sanctioning and disbursing hundreds of crores of rupees towards purchase of high end automobiles, fancy cars, private jets and even yachts. A bank, which was formed with the objective of engaging in social banking had clearly crossed the line, by financing the toys of rich boys and encouraging snobbish acquisition of assets that were unrelated to the business needs of the customer by any stretch of imagination.

The valuations of such high end assets posed unique problems of their own. The bank, which was barely able to assess proposals of home loans, mortgage loans, SME and the like, was called upon to assess exotic loan proposals, just to accommodate the defaulting borrower. The credit department of the bank, however much capable they be, were found to be ill equipped to assess proposals of such magnitude. Under the circumstances, all such proposals were sent to the Board for clearance, which the Board seemed to merrily clear without losing much sleep.

Valuations of such gizmos were best left to the specialists in the field. The fees charged by the valuers for their services were exorbitant, which the borrower was willing to pay by enhancing the loan amount suitably. The Board would clear such deviations, stating that more the loan quantum the better it is to the bank's bottom line by way of interest servicing. The borrower on the other hand, felt that the high interest or exorbitant valuation fees levied by the bank was inconsequential, as he had no intention of repaying the loan in the first place. The loans would tread themselves aimlessly to a black hole, on their way to becoming a case of quick mortality.

Had the bank not collapsed like a pack of cards, the no holds barred party would have continued for a little longer through constant ever greening and structuring. However, with the bank going down the tubes, all such cases had surfaced much in advance.

Though the bank had its loans covered through prime and collateral securities, they were merely book entries. In effect, the cost of maintaining such unusual assets in good condition was taking a toll on the bank's coffers, thereby further pushing the asking price of the assets.

When the entire world was going through recessionary times and cost cutting had become the mantra, no one was willing to loosen their purse strings. The result was telling on the bank's efforts to sell its high end assets. There were no takers for the Lexus, Lamborghini and Maserati or the fully loaded Yacht docked in the Arabian sea off the coast of Dona Paula near Panjim in Goa, or the the several Private Jets languishing and gathering dust at the hanger of Pawan Hans near Juhu in suburban Mumbai, with mounting overdues through uncleared rentals. The bank's failure was becoming a case study of worst practices in living memory, rather than best practices to be followed.

The bank also realised that all its efforts to auction the tainted assets were failing as no actual users were participating at such auctions. This was ascribed to the traditional Indian thought process of not purchasing any tainted asset. The logic being, if an asset had not brought prosperity or had actually brought ill luck to its past owners, it is better avoided.

Hence, at such drives, it was only the investors and grave diggers who would show their interest with an abysmally low quotation. These professionals knew that the bank was stressed and losing valuable time and, hence, would have no option but to let go of their prime assets at throwaway prices. A game of who would blink first was being played out between the parties. The vultures were in no hurry. They knew that sooner or later, the corpse of the bank would be available to them to devour at their own sweet time and asking price.

SECTION 03: Tips to Customers While Selecting a Bank

While some of the banks have come into criticism lately, investors need not adopt a knee jerk reaction. Though the failure of one bank is likely to rub off on the customer's perception of the other banks and have a temporary domino effect on the sector as a whole, this need not always be true in the case of all banks.

Depositors need to be discerning and decide for themselves what is right for them, based on merits, after seeking information from their bank and giving a score against each of the below mentioned points. If the depositor is satisfied with the final score, a decision can be taken based on the same.

Due care has been taken to ensure that this detailed self help guide is written in simple language, without using financial jargon or complicated terms, so that the financially less literate customers can arrive at a decision themselves. The aim is to facilitate customers to take informed decisions rather than rely on hearsay while investing their hard earned savings with any financial institution.

The investor should read each point carefully and give **1 mark** if it meets the expectation and a **0 mark** if it does not meet the expectation. If the cumulative total of the marks is more than 90%, the bank may be considered for investment.

Disclaimer: While all the points in the score card are important, in our view, the first two critical points along with 25 major points are to be taken seriously. Hence, even if the total marks obtained is over 90%, customer discretion is still advised, if the critical and major points are not met. They may well be considered as the **deal breakers**.

The author is bank agnostic and does not promote or reject any specific bank. He also recommends investors to follow prudent practices to spread their risk (investments) over many banks rather than place all their investments with just a few banks. Ignorance is often no excuse under law, more so, when the customers make their investment decisions.

The below points are designed to act as a guide to decision making. They are both macro and micro suggestions, however, no claim is made that the points are exhaustive or all inclusive.

Points to Ponder Before Investing in Fixed Deposits with Any Preferred Bank

The score card is detailed and includes all major points to be considered before investing. Your life savings are important. They will be relatively safe if you find out more about your bank. The below guide can help you.

If a banker is hesitant, and unable to provide information or a convincing answer to any of the critical and major questions, it may be better to avoid such a bank.

(Scoring pattern - 1 mark against each point for positive information and 0 mark for negative information)

Critical Points

1. Is the bank politically exposed?

(0 mark if the bank is known to have political links and 1 mark if the bank is not politically

exposed. PEP or Politically Exposed Persons are classified under a High Risk Category by the Regulator RBI)

2. Are the Chairman, Board of Directors, MD and CEO known for their integrity, reputation and transparency or do they have a questionable image as per the information available in the public domain?

(0 mark for known questionable image, 1 if they do not have any incriminating information against them in the public domain)

Major Points (1 to 25):

1. Whether name of the Chairman, Board of Directors, MD and CEO is prominently put up on the Bank's website/Branch Notice Board or is the Branch Manager willing to provide the information?

(0 mark if information is absent, 1 if it is provided)

2. Whether the bank has professional Directors with 2 experienced Bankers in its Board?

(0 mark for absence, 1 if Professional Directors are in the Board)

3. Whether all the crucial decision-making at the bank is taken through a collective committee approach or is vested with a single person in the Board/HO?

(1 for collective approach, 0 in case of single person)

4. Does the bank have working committees such as a Committee of Executives, Credit Committee, Audit Committee, IT Committee, Recovery and Legal Committee, etc.?

(0 for absence, 1 for presence of such committee based working)

5. Does the bank have documented financial and non-financial delegation of powers for officials working at the Head Office and Branches of the bank?

(0 for absence, 1 for presence of delegated powers)

6. Is the bank having a Risk Department headed by a Chief Risk Officer to prepare a detailed risk note on Credit, Market and Operational risks for all major loan proposals?

(0 for absence, 1 for presence)

7. Is the Loan Department of the bank working independently in accordance with the Credit Policy of the bank?

(0 for no, 1 for yes)

8. Are any Directors/Chairman part of the Loan Committee or are the Loan Proposals independently assessed by the Officers of the Loan Committee?

(0 if yes for the first part, 1 if yes for second part)

9. Does the bank have KYC and Loan Appraisal policies, wherein the income and repayment capacity of the borrower is given more weightage over the value of security?

(0 for absence, 1 for presence of such prudent policies)

10. Is the bank registered with rating agencies such as CIBIL, Experian, Equifax, CRIF Highmark, etc., and does the bank upload on these sites its loan data each month?

(0 for absence, 1 if bank is registered and uploads data)

11. Are large loan proposals referred by Directors/Agents/CA firms, etc., or are all the high value

loan proposals sourced by the bank's management themselves?

(0 for yes to first part and 1 for yes to second part)

12. When the Chairman and Board of Directors refer high value loan proposals, are they recusing themselves from participating in the appraisal and sanction process?

(0 if they participate in the process, 1 if they do not)

13. Is the bank monitoring the overdue loan position on a daily basis and does it have a team of officers in its Recovery Department to recover the overdue promptly?

(0 for absence, 1 for presence)

14. Is the bank conducting regular inspection of stocks and book debts of its borrowers? Does it have a team of qualified Officers to undertake this exercise?

(0 for absence, 1 for compliance and presence of a team)

15. Does the bank have a Core Banking Solution and are all its branches connected to the network? Is the CBS offered by a reputed and experienced IT company? Do all transactions get routed through

the Core Banking Software of the bank **or** does the bank hold data in an excel format outside the Core Banking Platform?

(1 if yes for first part and 0 if the bank holds some loan data in an excel format)

16. What was the RBI audit rating of the bank for the past 3 years? (A rating being high and D being low)

(1 if the rating is A, 0 for all other ratings)

17. Based on the audit rating and other parameters set by the RBI, is the bank certified by the RBI as Financially Sound and Well Managed (FS&WM)?

(1 if the bank is FS&WM, 0 if it is not)

18. Are the Gross and Net Non-Performing Assets (NPAs) of the bank well within the RBI norms?

(1 for yes, 0 if the NPA is beyond the RBI norms)

19. Does the provisioning by the bank sufficiently cover its NPAs?

(0 if provisioning is short and 1 if provisioning is adequate)

20. Has the bank ever been penalised by RBI or any restrictions been imposed on it by RBI?

(0 if it has been penalised, 1 if not penalised)

21. Is the bank paying premium on its deposits once every six months to the Deposit Insurance Credit Guarantee Corporation? Is a copy of the premium receipt on display?

(1 if DICGC premium is paid and copy of the premium receipt is furnished for viewing and 0 if it is not paid or available for viewing by the customer)

22. Do you find the bank to be offering unusually high interest rates on its deposits in comparison with similar banks?

(0 if the rates are high in comparison and 1 if rates are equal or less than competing banks)

23. Does the bank charge very high interest rates on its loans in comparison with the competing banks?

(0 if interest rates on loans are very high and thereby attracting low quality assets, 1 if rates are not high or are similar with those of the other banks)

24. Does the bank have well laid down single party and group exposure norms under its Credit Policy? Is the majority of the loan disbursed to a single party?

(0 if bank does not have such norms and 1 if it has such norms and follows the same)

25. Is the bank giving high value loans to Corporates or businesses run/referred to by Directors?

(1 if bank does not have such loans in its books and 0 if it has a large percentage of such loans in its books)

Ancillary Points (1 to 42):

1. Does the bank have a policy of conducting independent Management Audits by a CA firm of Key Departments at its HO, at least once in two years?

(0 for absence, 1 if Management Audit is conducted)

2. Did you find the Branch Manager and Officers to be capable of conducting an in depth 'know the borrower' exercise and were seen to be doing their preliminary due diligence?

(0 for absence of capability, 1 for presence)

3. Is the bank profit making or has it been incurring losses during the past 3 years?

(1 for profit making, 0 for losses in past 3 years)

4. Does the bank declare dividends year on year to its share-holders?

(1 for yes, 0 for no dividend declared year on year)

5. Does the bank have a healthy 'Credit to Deposit ratio' exceeding 60%?

(1 if CD ratio is over 60% and 0 if it is less than 60%)

6. Does the bank have an active Treasury Department with access to NDS - OM?

(0 for absence of active Treasury Department and 1 if it has)

7. Do the bank's internal and statutory auditors regularly audit the Credit and Treasury Department?

(1 for yes, 0 for no)

8. Is the return on investment earned by the Treasury Department for the past year through its investments/trading in Treasury Bills and Government Securities commensurate with the cost of funds/deposits of the bank?

(1 if Treasury returns are equal or more than deposit rates and 0 if returns are less than the deposit rates)

9. Does the bank maintain Statutory Liquidity Ratio and Cash Reserve Ratio as mandated by the regulator or has it been penalised for any default in maintaining the same?

(0 for default in CRR/SLR and 1 for maintaining CRR/SLR with no penalty for default)

10. Does the bank have a designated Nodal/Principal Officer (NO and PO) to interact with the regulators?

(0 if the bank does not have and 1 if it has a NO and PO)

11. Is the bank having an escalation matrix to respond to customer complaints within a pre-accepted, turn-around time for the same? Is it displayed at the branch/website?

(1 if bank has it and has displayed the same and 0 if it does not have)

12. Is the bank having a CASA base of 30% and above or is it largely dependent on high cost Term Deposits?

(0 if CASA is less than 30% of total deposits, 1 if CASA is 30% or more)

13. Is the Net Interest Margin over 3%? (NIM is the difference between interest on

deposits and interest on loans after factoring operational costs).

(0 if NIM is less than 3% and 1 if NIM is more than 3%)

14. Does the bank have a Transfer Price Rate to pay branches generating more deposits and less loans?

(0 if the bank does not have a TPR and 1 if it has a TPR)

15. Does the bank's loan book contain more of small value loans or does it have more of high value loans?

(1 if the majority of loan customers are individuals, small and medium establishments and 0 if they are largely high value corporate loans)

16. Is the bank having a concentration of giving large loans to a particular sector or industry or to Commercial Real Estate Co's, thus exposing it to sectoral risks?

(1 if it does not have such exposure and 0 if it has such concentration)

17. Does the bank have a policy of recruiting officers from the market or does it employ

friends and relatives referred by the Board of Directors?

(1 if it has a policy of recruiting from the market and 0 if it has been recruiting internally)

18. Are the Staff, Officers and Managers regularly sent for training to various institutions such as College of Agricultural Banking/Vaikunth Mehta College of Banking or independent training faculties?

(0 if training needs are not provided and 1 if they are)

19. When was the bank established and what has been its branch and business growth since its inception?

(0 if bank has remained stagnant through the years, 1 if it has steadily grown over the years since its inception)

20. Does the bank have an offsite Data Center, Data Recovery and Business Continuity Plan (DC, DR and BCP) to meet exigencies?

(1 if it has an offsite DC, DR and BCP, 0 if it does not)

21. Does the bank serve just one community or does it have a more cosmopolitan and broad based clientele?

(0 if it only serves one community, 1 if it serves all)

22. How has the industrial relationship of the bank been with its staff and union?

(0 if there has been a strike during the past 3 years and 1 if the industrial relations have been cordial)

23. Does the bank have a front and back office culture and a wall between the two functions, viz., sourcing loan proposals and scrutinising/assessing the same?

(0 if it does not have and 1 if it has such front and back offices and hands off arrangement between the two)

24. Is the bank having a well laid down organization and reporting structure and is it process driven (as opposed to person driven) in its day to day functions?

(0 for absence and 1 for presence of such a practice)

25. Does the Branch Manager have powers to debit Profit and Loss Account to refund charges and income?

(0 if Branch Manager has such powers and 1 if not)

26. Does the bank practice a 6 eye principle in all its transactions? Does it require a Maker/Checker and Authorizer to put through all its large value transactions?

(1 if the bank has such controls and 0 if it does not)

27. Is the bank cost conscious or is known to spend heavily on promotions/advertisements/campaigns?

(1 for yes to first part and 0 if yes to the second part)

28. Does the bank have the practice of maintaining minutes and resolutions of all its Committee and Board Meeting proceedings?

(1 for maintaining the records and 0 for not maintaining)

29. Does the bank file a Cash Transaction Report and Suspicious Transaction Report (CTR/STR) periodically with the Financial Intelligence

Unit (FIU) in a seamless manner right from its CBS?

(1 for filing CTR/STR with FIU and 0 for not filing)

30. Are the Chairman and Board of Directors engaged in businesses which are likely to result in conflict of interest with the working of the bank?

(0 for clash of interest and 1 for no conflict of interest)

31. Are the Board Members and Chairman known to have related party transactions with the bank and if so, are such details reported periodically to the regulator?

(0 if such details are not reported and 1 if there are related party transaction and the same are reported periodically to the regulators)

32. Does the bank follow, in letter and spirit, the Dos and Don'ts as laid down by the RBI for the working of the bank and its top Management and Board?

(0 if it does not, 1 if it follows the Dos and Don'ts in letter and spirit)

33. Has the bank been using the provisions of the National Company Law Tribunal (NCLT) and

The Securitisation and Reconstruction of Financial Assets and Enforcement of Securities Interest Act, 2002 (SARFAESI Act) to recover its Non-Performing Assets and Bad Loans well in time?

(1 if bank uses NCLT and SARFAESI and 0 if it does not)

34. Does the bank have an email culture of giving and receiving all sensitive financial instructions through emails or are these done over the phone by the Management and Board?

(1 if emails are used as the documented mode of communication and 0 if oral instructions are resorted to)

35. Is important data such as Share Capital, Reserves, Deposits, Loans, NPAs, Profit, Dividend, Number of Employees, etc., displayed at the Branch?

(1 if they are displayed publicly and 0 if they are not)

36. Is the RBI licence copy and Abridged version of the Financials displayed at the Branch notice board/website or available for scrutiny with the Branch Manager?

(1 if they are displayed and 0 if they are not provided)

37. Does the bank secure all its vouchers, critical loan documents and property related papers in a fire proof filing cabinet within its own premises or at an offsite location, and hold the same safely in accordance with the law of limitation?

(1 if docs are in a fire proof filing cabinet and held as per the law of limitation and 0 if not)

38. Does the bank offer digital and internet banking, facilitating customers to make financial transactions with firewalls?

(1 if the bank offers the facility and 0 if it does not)

39. Does bank have a panel of highly reputed valuers to assess the value of collaterals and lawyers to conduct encumbrance search of the collateral mortgaged?

(0 for absence, 1 for presence)

40. Does the bank have documented policies and monthly meetings by the top management to review and deal with the below?

Anti-corruption policy, Whistle blower policy, Sexual harassment policy, Gifts (giving or receiving), Travel and Entertainment policy, Customer grievance addressal, Escalation policy,

Contributions to and from political parties or politically exposed personnel.
(0 for absence of the policies and 1 for their presence)

41. Is the bank having risk categorisation of its customers into Low, Medium and High Risk categories as mandated by the RBI?
(0 for absence of the policy and 1 for its presence)

42. Does the bank's Core Banking Solution allot Unique Customer Identification Code (UCIC) as mandated by the RBI to link all the accounts of a customer or a combination of customers to the respective UCIC, to be able to identify and restrict/dedupe accounts held by the same customer across all the branches of the bank, at any given point of time?
(0 for absence of UCIC and 1 for its presence)

43. Does the bank have an in-house legal and recovery team?
(0 for absence and 1 for its presence)

(The questionnaire is designed to guide and help the common public arrive at their investment decisions with their chosen bank. No part of it is to be copied, transmitted or reproduced for commercial purposes, without the written permission of the author/publishers).

Annexure

Total score obtained for the bank/s that are considered for investment:

Critical points

(Ideal score should be 2 out of 2)

Major Points

(Ideal score should be at least 20 out of 25)

Ancillary Points

(Ideal score can be as per individual perception)

Suggested Steps for the Regulator's Consideration

SECTION 04

Below are some of the suggestions to the regulator to ensure that future failure of banks is prevented, through a series of prompt actions and by upping their ante so as to anticipate challenging situations and take remedial measures to contain the damage, well before the situation spins out of control.

As customers should not take impulsive decisions to pull out their funds just because one bank fails, similarly, the regulator also should not adopt a knee jerk reaction or resort to taking extreme measures in the case of every bank, for avoiding the fear of creating panic amongst the depositors and a resultant run on the bank. The decision to admonish, penalise and pass strictures should be taken deftly and in a thoughtful manner, to protect the confidence of the customers.

Get under the direct supervision of all those institutions and entities that have the word 'Bank' in their name and are in the business of mobilising deposits from people. When a bank fails, it is natural for the regulator to get blamed fairly and squarely for failing to show the red flag when indications started appearing that all was not well at the bank. If regulators fail to detect such warning signals well in time, they will surely get blamed by the common public. Hence, it is imperative that all banking institutions come under the direct supervision of the regulator.

Conduct mandatory inspections of banks annually, based on pre-determined parameters, instead of carrying it out once in 2 years for banks rated A or for those which fall under the Financially Sound and Well Managed status. The once in two year audit leaves a large time frame for some of the unscrupulous banks to indulge in wrongdoings. If the regulator has resource constraints, a checklist can be provided to the CA Institute, asking them to shortlist members to carry out the inspection as per the scope given by the regulator. Selection of the CAs can be done jointly by the institute and the regulator, as per strict Fit and Proper norms for the selected CA/CA firms.

To help the common public and customers understand the rating, simply rank the bank as outstanding, good or bad, without making it complex with jargons.

Alternatively, to help the uninformed customers to know the ratings easily and without requiring to undertake too much analysis, give each bank a colour code, viz., green for outstanding, yellow for good and red for poor.

It should be made compulsory for the bank to prominently display the colour code awarded to it, on its branch signage, letter heads, email communications, visiting cards, notices, posters, pamphlets and other such marketing/sales collaterals, shared with the customers. The present parameters of the bank should be printed on leaflets and mandatorily shared with walk-in customers at the branches. As and when the colour code undergoes a change, the same should also be updated in the above listed documents and informed to the customers accordingly.

The abridged version of the previous year's financials and the regulator's rating along with its implications, in an easy to understand, uniform language, cleared by the regulator, should be printed behind the statement of accounts issued to the deposit holders.

After every inspection, banks should be made to mandatorily come up with public notices in at least 2 newspapers, one of which should be a vernacular newspaper, explaining the rating awarded to the bank and its implications.

Letters should be sent to all the customers, duly signed by the Chairman and CEO, informing them of the rating awarded to the bank and its full implications in terms of benefits or the inherent risks the ratings imply.

Each branch should undertake customer meetings after every rating exercise, to inform the customers at such meets about the bank's ratings and its impact. The minutes of the same should be maintained at the branch.

Every bank should mandatorily have dedicated guardian Director/s assigned to each branch or a cluster of branches. Such Directors should be made accountable for the working of the branch/es under their purview, along with the respective Branch Manager/s, Top Management and Board of the bank.

Each member, desirous of contesting for elections to the Board of the bank, should prequalify through a Fit and Proper criteria, laid down by the regulator.

The fit and proper filing should be made compulsory for each Director, for every year during the tenure of the Board. Explanations for any huge variance need to be sought.

In case of large NPAs during the tenure of the present Board, permission to hold fresh elections should be deferred till the present Board brings the NPAs to the levels stipulated by the regulator.

The assets of those desirous of contesting for a position in the Board, should be made public on the eve of their contesting and at the end of every year of their tenure, after they have filed their tax returns.

The asset and ITR details of the Directors should be made available for viewing at the branch or HO, if and when the same is demanded by any interested customer/s.

Sitting fees of the Directors should be fixed at the first meeting of the new board immediately after the elections, and the CEO should get the same approved by the regulator. No Director should be permitted to offer their services Pro Bono, and such an offer would not, in any case, release them from their implied obligations and responsibilities. The same should be conveyed to all the Directors.

Delegation of Financial and Non-Financial powers of the top management and the Board should be documented, with consent in writing taken from the respective Officer/Manager/Board Member. Such delegation of powers should be filed with the regulator, along with a note justifying the reasons, experience and qualifications of the Director made to Chair/Head or participate in a particular Committee.

In case any bank is awarded a poor rating for 2 consecutive years, it should not be permitted to lend or accept fresh deposits or renew existing deposits, until the bank corrects the reasons for which it was given a poor rating.

It should be made mandatory for the bank to include the audit ratings awarded to it, in the forthcoming annual report.

If a bank is awarded a poor rating for two consecutive years or does not earn the FSWM status for two consecutive years, such banks should be placed under prompt corrective action by the regulator along with enhanced strictures.

If a bank gets a poor rating thrice during the term of the Board, such Board Members should be barred from contesting future elections to any public office. A notice, giving the names of such banks and their Board Members, may be inserted in local newspapers for the information of the general public.

Dos and Don'ts as prescribed by the regulator should be accepted and signed on stamp papers of appropriate value by the incoming Board Members. Any future violations should attract financial penalty, loss of directorship or even a prison term, depending upon the seriousness of the lapses and its financial ramifications.

Any bank that voluntarily comes forward to take over a sick bank, should be awarded tax sops for a period of 3 to 5 years. All help to such banks in converting the failed bank into a Small Finance Bank, should be offered.

Directors should disclose, every year, the details of high value loan customers and staff members referred/introduced by them.

Any borrower account introduced by the Director or any other official of the bank, should be mandatorily made to recuse from attending meetings where the customer's loan proposal is taken up for discussion for either sanction or renewal.

Asset Liability Committee (ALCO) meetings should be conducted only by the management staff. Directors should not be included in such committees as per the extant directive.

Banks that voluntarily constitute the Board of Management with clearly defined roles and responsibilities of the BoM members, should be commended by the regulator. The Board and Management of such banks should be given due credit for attempting to professionalise the workings at their banks. RBI notification of the same should be released to make a positive example of such banks.

Banks that comply with the requirements of getting themselves transformed into a SFB, should be offered all help by the regulator. If any such bank voluntarily considers taking the leap, the regulator should take cognizance of the same and provide all professional help as well as commend such a step through its notifications, for other banks in the ecosystem to emulate.

RBI to have an active database and profile of professional bankers interested in offering professional help to the Co-operative banks to improve their internal processes and SOPs. Co-op banks, desirous of seeking help, to be provided the database of such bankers so that the banks and the professionals take the initiative forward without any obligations to the regulator. Both, the regulator and the bank's management and Board, should demonstrate a willingness to seek help from professionals. The openness to enlist help can assist in bringing best practices to the industry.

In addition to the annual inspection exercise, RBI to have a team of auditors designated as the flying squad, to pay surprise visits to banks that are borderline cases and could slip into poor rating in the absence of routine monitoring. Such monitoring can also be outsourced to the CA institute, to be handled by its qualified CA members, jointly selected by both the regulator and the CA institute.

Instead of recruiting Retired bankers as GMs and CEOs, RBI to counsel Co-operative banks to employ younger bankers to the critical posts, so as to ensure that industry best practices are introduced and longer innings by such bankers are played at their respective banks. This initiative will help the Co-Op banks have continuity of leadership over a longer tenure.

The RBI should also recommend to the Co-operative banks to introduce a combination of fixed and variable pay (linked to performance) for the key management personnel. Although, non achieving of the targets should not result in fault finding or witch hunting exercises by the Board.

The non-executive Chairman to be restricted from participating or in indulging/managing the day to day operational matters and business of the bank, as per the extant RBI's guidelines on the Dos and Don'ts for the Chairman and the Board. For reiteration, the posters giving the Dos and Don'ts should be prominently displayed at the Board Room/Corporate Office of the Bank.

The DICGC cover premium of banks with Poor audit rating and non FSWM status to be increased in accordance with the risk perception and rating.

A single point ombudsman at the regulator's office to be appointed to deal with any negative information shared by customers/employees of the bank. If the same is found correct, the informer to be awarded suitably. Name of the informer should be kept discreet. The ombudsman's contact details to be placed prominently at the branch/office and on the bank's website.

Steps should be taken to work closely with the Registrar's office at the various states and train the team in conducting effective audit of different banks, more particularly the non-scheduled and unit banks under their domain, with emphasis on checking whether the banks have fully complied with the past remarks and recommendations by the regulator.

Scheduled banks getting penalised more than twice or those with poor audit ratings twice in the past five years or not qualifying for the Financially Sound and Well Managed status during the past 2 consecutive years, will automatically qualify for penalty, which includes placing such banks under Prompt Corrective Action.

Make it mandatory for banks to have a Chief Compliance Officer and a Chief Risk Officer. Every loan proposal, beyond a pre-determined value, to compulsorily have both compliance and a risk note observation and a subsequent sign off by the Board, either accepting the observations of the CCO and CRO or over riding it at their own risk and responsibility.

At each branch office, the BMs cabin and those cubicles at the Corporate Office, Loans Department, CEO's cabin, Chairman's cabin and the board room, to mandatorily have CCTV installation. Internal and external auditors to conduct surprise sample checks to verify whether the same is operational or not.

Make it mandatory to have transfers of key officials, at least once every 3 to 5 years, to avoid concentration risks in few individuals, simultaneously creating bench strength for succession planning, enhancing job knowledge and excellence, uniformly.

Banks to be asked to mandatorily invest pre-determined man hours and financial budget per employee to meet the training needs of such staff and officers. In-house classroom/training college to be set up for simulation purposes. Professional trainers to be invited to train on various areas of banking as well as soft skills, customer services, communication techniques, etiquettes, corporate governance, inter-personal skills, etc. Banks to be advised to create bench strength and succession plan for key departments.

Concept of mandatory core leave to be introduced, whereby each staff member and officer would be required to avail fixed days of leave every year. This will eliminate the indispensability factor as well as assist in bringing to light serious lapses that may exist in the working of the said official / department.

The RBI inspection team to be briefed to go beyond financials. Based on their discussions with the Bank Management, it should record findings about various procedural breaches at the bank along with observations about any impropriety noticed by the IOs. The RBI inspection team to be accessible and open communication channels, without diluting their core responsibilities in any way. On the last day of the yearly inspection, in addition to meeting the Chairman and the Board of Directors, the RBI Inspecting Officials to also mandatorily meet the Branch Managers and Departmental Heads for a briefing about their observations and suggest dos and don'ts as well as necessary steps that they need to take for the overall improvement of the bank.

The RBI officials to visit banks that have consistently weak ratings, in their effort to reach out to the team across the bank, including the union representatives to discuss and suggest ways to formulate an action plan with everyone's buy in, in order to improve the health of their bank.

To make it mandatory to have monthly staff meetings at the branches and departments as well as customer meets as a PR initiative to explain the bank's key features to them.

Conduct one day workshops, exclusively for the Chairman and CEO of banks having poor audit ratings. This will help to educate them on the steps that they need to urgently take and seek help that is available from the regulator to bring about improvements in their bank.

Suggest to banks that have been consistently performing well on all parameters, to visit selected banks that need improvement, with a view to share their mantra for achieving consistent success, for the benefit of the weak banks in the sector.

Impress upon banks that need improvement, to invite professionals to conduct Management Audits and come up with areas of immediate concern along with steps needed for improvement.

Get system and cyber audit done by a professional entity having extensive domain knowledge, certifications and an eye for detail, to identify the latest forms of cybercrime and online frauds as well as steps to prevent the same.

Set up a centralised processing cell to objectively assess all high value loans, independent of the sourcing team and without any direct interaction with the customers, to lay stress on systems and processes, rather than make functions person dependent.

While the scope of work of the regulator's inspection team, when conducting the inspection, is to go through the data provided by the bank, it cannot absolve itself completely when a bank shuts down. Though, it is not expected of the inspection team to conduct a forensic audit as a matter of routine, but going by the past records at some of the banks, the RBI inspectors should be briefed to conduct enhanced due diligence and the inspection team should be educated about what to look for at such banks by keeping their analytical minds sharp to pick up any aberration and warning signals.

The RBI may not have all the answers, but when things go wrong, a lay person will be inclined to blame the regulator. The RBI should take proactive steps to avoid such instances and not wait for the next scam to happen to implement corrective steps. Punishments and penalties should be stringent and the fear of law should be made amply clear to the scamsters and fraudsters.

The regulator should take cognizance of the private and confidential letters from the CEOs and top ranking officials of the banks and not procrastinate in taking timely, informed decisions in case it has merits. In the interest of the sector, the regulator should encourage vigilant bankers working in each bank, to blow the whistle when they see wrongdoing on a massive scale. The name and contact details of such whistle blowers should be protected and not made public to avoid risk to their life. If the allegation of the whistle blower is proved correct, the regulator should consider rewarding him/her. During the yearly inspection, the IO should network over lunch with a cross section of staff and officers to pick up any dissenting voice.

When a bank is asked to stop operations, some unsubstantiated information is bound to float in the press and social media. To kill such rumours, the RBI should open up communication channels and take proactive steps of issuing daily or weekly news bulletins on the proceedings of such banks, to assuage the apprehensions of its depositors. This will generate goodwill and not give an impression that the regulator is resorting to stone walling the request for information from the common public and the depositor community. The regulator should make efforts to demonstrate its willingness to engage, be transparent and prompt in sharing information.

When restrictions are imposed on a bank, the RBI should preferably appoint an administrator at the bank, who has PR skills, in-depth knowledge of commercial banking as well as loads of empathy for the average customer. If the administrator needs professional help, the same should be provided from the database of commercial bankers, which the RBI has in its archives.

When a bank fails, the RBI needs to swing into action in a time bound manner to ring fence the assets of the bank, including the hard collateral security of its borrowers. Conservative 'distress sale value' to be sought from multiple agencies. DICGC to offer a bail-out package and make available funds to the extent of the distress sale value of the assets/collaterals, to immediately pay out in full the small depositors. Upon realisation of sale proceeds of the assets and collaterals, the same to be adjusted against the bail-out package rendered by DICGC.

As the scamsters come up with newer ways of defrauding a bank, the RBI should update their Inspecting Officials with latest case studies in the industry. The IOs should be trained to spot/undertake volume and velocity checks as well as identify any abnormality, although the routine parameters may well be satisfactory. Any large investments in property at an unrealistic price range or loans that are regularly nearer to the single party exposure limits, should be investigated to spot related party transactions. Similarly, large number of small ticket loans that escape the radar of the IO due to these loans falling below the threshold levels, should be thoroughly investigated to spot layering and structuring to camouflage the ultimate beneficiary of such small loans.

All the regulatory directives issued during the past year, should be discussed by the IO with the top management of the banks for its thorough implementation.

Even before commencing inspection of the banks, the regulator should counsel the Inspection Officials team to also look for a spike in a large number of small MSME/Unsecured Loans, as well as those through the Dealer Networks, Business Correspondents, Salary Loans, etc. They should conduct a random sample inspection of the portfolio, the process followed, the sanctioning/ratifying authorities, documentation, collateral security, if any, payment track record, KYC checks, etc., to assess the risk, and search for any abnormal pattern should be undertaken.

Those borrowers enjoying working capital limits, should be insisted to maintain their Current Account with the bank, so as to enable the bank to realise the receivables and avoid any attempt by the borrowers to divert the loans for purposes other than the end use stated in their loan application.

BANKING ABBREVIATIONS

How many times do we get to hear unfamiliar terms and jargons used by bankers? All over the world, bankers are known to use abbreviations which could unsettle and thoroughly confuse their customers. Hence, for the benefit of the readers, some of the abbreviations in alphabetical order are decoded here.

AGM	–	Assistant General Manager
ALCO	–	Asset Liability Committee
ALM	–	Asset Liability Management
AM	–	Assistant Manager
AML	–	Anti Money Laundering
AO	–	Administrative Office

API	–	Application Programming Interface
APP	–	Application (for Mobile users)
AQB	–	Average Quarterly Balance
ASBA	–	Applications Supported by Blocked Amount
ATM	–	Automated Teller Machine
AVP	–	Assistant Vice President
BCP	–	Business Continuity Plan
BD	–	Book Debts
BEN	–	Beneficiary
BHIM	–	Bharat Interface for Money
BIA	–	Bankruptcy and Insolvency Act
BIFR	–	Board for Industrial and Financial Reconstruction
BL	–	Bill of Lading
BM	–	Branch Manager
BoM	–	Board of Management
BPLR	–	Benchmark Prime Lending Rate
BPR	–	Business Process Re-engineering

BR	–	Bills Receivable
BR Act	–	Banking Regulation Act
BS	–	Balance Sheet
BSBDA	–	Basic Savings Bank Deposit Account
BSE	–	Bombay Stock Exchange
CASA	–	Current Account Savings Account
CB	–	Corporate Banking
CBS	–	Core Banking Solution
CC	–	Cash Credit
CC	–	Credit Card
CCIL	–	Clearing Corporation of India Ltd.
CCM	–	Credit Committee Meeting
CD	–	Certificate of Deposit/Credit to Deposit Ratio
CDF	–	Currency Declaration Form
CEO	–	Chief Executive Officer
CFO	–	Chief Financial Officer
CG	–	Corporate Guarantee
CGM	–	Chief General Manager

CHRO	–	Chief Human Resources Officer
CI	–	Cash Incentive
CM	–	Chief Manager
CO	–	Compliance Officer
CO and HO	–	Corporate Office; Head Office
COO	–	Chief Operating/ Operations Officer
CP and CS	–	Conditions Precedent and Conditions Subsequent
CRAR	–	Capital to Risk Assets Ratio
CRE	–	Commercial Real Estate
CRO	–	Chief Risk Officer
CRR	–	Cash Reserve Ratio
CSR	–	Corporate Social Responsibility
CTO	–	Chief Technology Officer
CTR	–	Cash Transaction Report
CTS	–	Cheque Truncation System
DBA	–	Data Base Administrator
DC	–	Data Center
DC	–	Debit Card

DC	–	Documentary Credit
DD	–	Demand Draft
DD	–	Duty Drawback
DEMAT	–	Dematerialization (of physical documents in electronic form, e.g. Share Certificates)
DGM	–	Deputy General Manager
DICGC	–	Deposit Insurance Credit Guarantee Corporation
DIN	–	Director Identification Number
DMS	–	Document Management System
DPDs	–	Days Past Due
DR	–	Disaster Recovery
DSCR	–	Debt Service Coverage Ratio
DTAA	–	Double Taxation Avoidance Agreement
ECB	–	External Commercial Borrowings
ECS	–	Electronic Clearing Service
ED	–	Enforcement Directorate
EMI	–	Equated Monthly Instalment

EOW	–	Economic Offences Wing
EVP	–	Executive Vice President
FATF	–	Financial Action Tax Force
FCCB	–	Foreign Currency Convertible Bonds
FCNR	–	Foreign Currency Non Resident
FCRA	–	Foreign Contribution Regulation Act
FD	–	Fixed Deposit
FEDAI	–	Foreign Exchange Dealers' Association of India
FEMA	–	Foreign Exchange Management Act
FERA	–	Foreign Exchange Regulation Act
FIG	–	Financial Institutions Group
FIMMDA	–	The Fixed Income Money Market and Derivatives Association of India
FINMIN	–	Finance Ministry
FIU	–	Financial Intelligence Unit
FOREX	–	Foreign Exchange
FS&WM Bank	–	Financially Sound and Well Managed Bank

FSR	–	Financial Sector Reforms
FX	–	Foreign Exchange
GI	–	General Insurance
GM	–	General Manager
G-Sec	–	Government Securities
HL	–	Home Loan
HO	–	Head Office
HOD	–	Head of the Department
HRD	–	Human Resources Development
HRMS	–	Human Resources Management System
IB	–	Investment Banking
IBA	–	Indian Banks Association
IBR	–	Inter-Bank Reconciliation
IFSC	–	Indian Financial System Code
IMPS	–	Immediate Payment Service
IO	–	Inspecting Official
IRDA	–	Insurance Regulatory and Development Authority
IRDP	–	Integrated Rural Development Programme
IT	–	Information Technology

ITR	–	Income Tax Return
JLG	–	Joint Liability Group
LAP	–	Loan Against Property
LC	–	Letter of Credit
LI	–	Life Insurance
LOC	–	Letter of Comfort
LOD	–	List of Documents
LOI	–	Letter of Intent
LORO	–	Theirs (in Italian language)
LOU	–	Letter of Undertaking
LR	–	Lorry Receipt
LTV	–	Loan to Value
MA	–	Management Audit
MANCOM	–	Management Committee
MGNREGA	–	Mahatma Gandhi National Rural Employment Guarantee Act
MCLR	–	Marginal Cost of funds based Lending Rate
MD	–	Managing Director
MDR	–	Merchant Discount Rate
MF	–	Mutual Funds
MICR	–	Magnetic Ink Character Recognition

ML	–	Mortgage Loan
MSME	–	Micro, Small and Medium Enterprise
NACH	–	National Automated Clearing House
NREGA	–	National Rural Employment Guarantee Act
NB	–	Net Banking
NCLT	–	National Company Law Tribunal
NDS-OM	–	Negotiated Dealing System Order Matching
NEFT	–	National Electronic Funds Transfer
NI Act	–	Negotiable Instruments Act
NIM	–	Net Interest Margin
NO	–	Nodal Officer
NOSTRO	–	Ours (in Italian language)
NPA	–	Non Performing Asset
NPCI	–	National Payments Corporation of India
NPS	–	The National Pension System
NRE	–	Non Resident External

NRI	–	Non Resident Indian
NRO	–	Non Resident Ordinary
NSDL	–	National Securities Depository Ltd.
NSE	–	National Stock Exchange
OCI	–	Overseas Citizen of India
OD	–	Over Draft
PAN	–	Permanent Account Number
P&L	–	Profit and Loss
PB	–	Pass Book
PB	–	Phone Banking
PC	–	Packing Credit
PCA	–	Prompt Corrective Action
PDCs	–	Post Dated Cheques
PE	–	Private Equity
PEP	–	Politically Exposed Persons
PFRDA	–	Pension Fund Regulatory and Development Authority
PPP	–	Public Private Participation
P2P	–	Peer to Peer/Person to Person
PG	–	Personal Guarantee
PIO	–	Person of Indian Origin
PIS	–	Portfolio Investment Scheme

PL	–	Personal Loan
PLR	–	Prime Lending Rate
PMS	–	Portfolio Management Services
PO	–	Pay Order
PO	–	Principle Officer
POS	–	Point of Sale
PP	–	Post Parcel
PPS	–	Positive Pay System
PRO	–	Public Relation Officer
PSU	–	Public Sector Undertaking
QR Code	–	Quick Response Code
RB	–	Retail Banking
RD	–	Recurring Deposit
RECON	–	Reconciliation
REPO	–	Repurchase Agreement
RLLR	–	Repo Linked Lending Rate
ROC	–	Registrar of Companies
RR	–	Railway Receipt
RTGS	–	Real Time Gross Settlement
RuPay	–	Rupee (Indian Rupees) Payment
SARFAESI Act	–	Securitisation and Reconstruction of Financial

		Assets and Enforcement of Securities Interest Act
SBLC	–	Standby Letter of Credit
SEBI	–	Securities and Exchange Board of India Ltd.
SEPUP	–	Self Employment Programme for the Urban Poor
SFB	–	Small Finance Bank
SFIO	–	Serious Fraud Investigation Office
SFMS	–	Structured Financial Messaging System
SGM	–	Senior General Manager
SLG	–	Self Help Group
SLR	–	Statutory Liquidity Ratio
SME	–	Small and Medium Establishments
SOP	–	Standard Operating Procedure
STR	–	Suspicious Transaction Report
SVP	–	Senior Vice President

SWIFT	–	Society for world-wide inter-bank financial telecommunication
T+1	–	Transaction plus 1 day
TAT	–	Turn Around Time
T-Bills	–	Treasury Bills
TDR	–	Term Deposit Receipt
TL	–	Term Loan
TReDS	–	Trade Receivables e-Discounting System
TT	–	Telex Transfer
UBD	–	Usance Bills Discounting
UCB	–	Urban Cooperative Bank
UCIC	–	Uniform Customer Identification Code
UCPDC	–	Uniform Customs and Practices Documentary Credit
UIDAI	–	The Unique Identification Authority of India
UPI	–	Unified Payment Interface
VOSTRO	–	Yours (in Italian language)
VP	–	Vice President
VPA	–	Virtual Payment Address

SPECIMEN ORGANOGRAM OF AN IDEAL FULL SERVICE RETAIL COMMERCIAL BANK

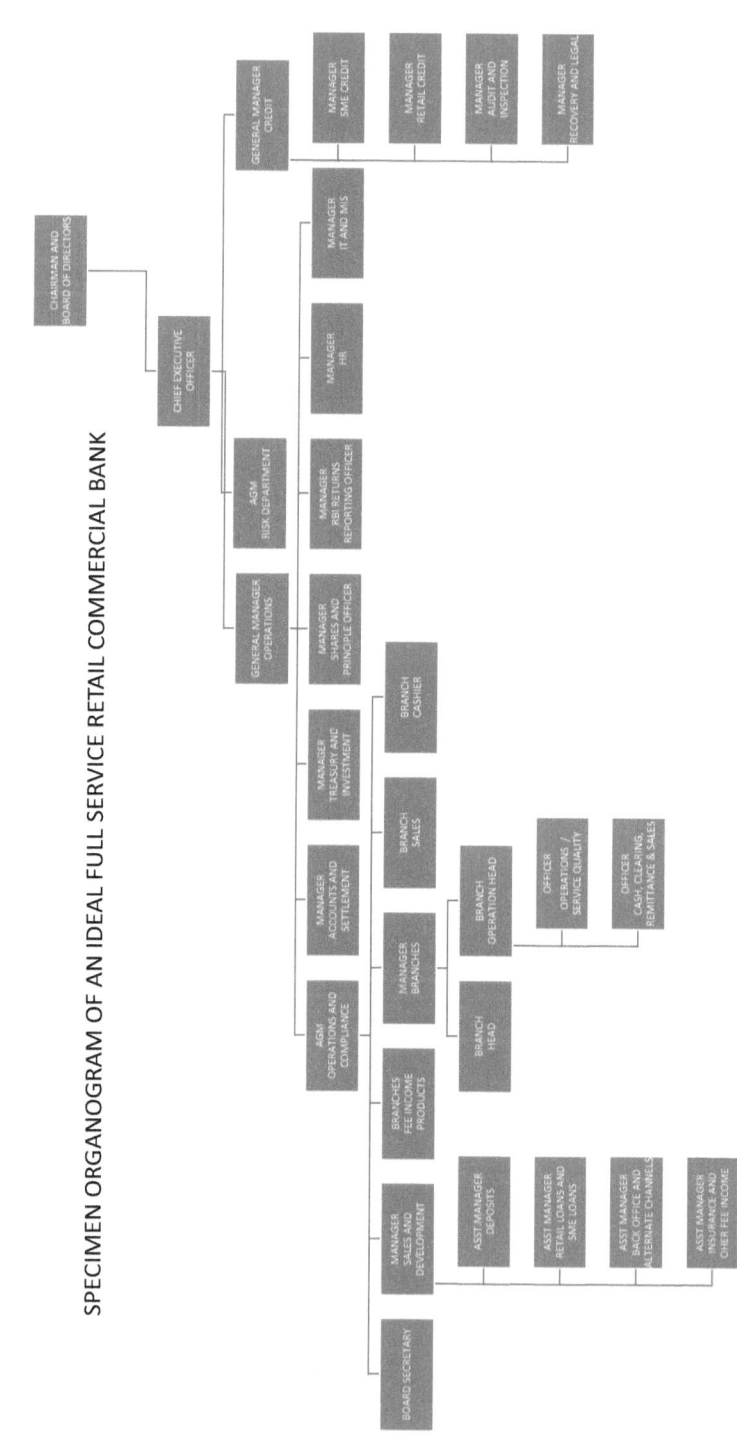

ABOUT THE AUTHOR

Chaitanya* was born and educated in Mumbai. He belongs to a family of bankers and started his banking career in 1980, while still pursuing graduation from the University of Mumbai.

In a career spanning 4 decades, he has worked and been associated with some of the finest Public Sector Banks, Foreign Banks in India, International Banks in the Middle East & UK, Payment Gateways, Co-Operative Banks & Fintechs in India.

---

* Chaitanya is the pen name of the author.

During his career, he has launched some of the trend setting retail banking products for the domestic market as well as investment products for the Non Resident Indians based overseas.

He has helped banks by introducing robust processes, new products, fee income streams and trained staff to be more proactive and process driven. He has also helped to professionalise the Board and adhere to regulatory norms.

He currently offers business process re-engineering services to banks desiring to improve their internal processes. He has trained hundreds of bankers and continues to train professional bankers and students, interested in taking up banking as their career.

http://www.bankonus.in

http://www.schoolofbanking.in

www.ingramcontent.com/pod-product-compliance
Lightning Source LLC
Chambersburg PA
CBHW020733180526
45163CB00001B/213